Travellers Wine Guide

Spain

Travellers Wine Guide

Spain

Desmond Begg

Photographs by Francesco Venturi

WAYMARK

The *Travellers Wine Guides*
were conceived and produced by
Philip Clark Limited
53 Calton Avenue, London SE21 7DF, UK

Designed by Keith Faulkner Publishing
Limited

Edited by Ros Mair

Photographs by Francesco Venturi
(except where otherwise credited)

Maps by Andrew Green and Simon Green

Published in Great Britain by
Waymark Publications, an imprint of
the Automobile Association, Fanum House,
Basingstoke, Hampshire RG21 2EA

© Philip Clark Limited, 1989
First published 1989

ISBN 0 86145 762 5

Phototypeset in Great Britain by
Input Typesetting Limited

Colour reproduction in Singapore by
Columbia Offset Limited

Printed and bound in Hong Kong

ACKNOWLEDGEMENT

The author and publisher
would particularly like to
thank **Wines from Spain**
for their help with the
research and planning of
this book.

PHOTO CREDITS

Antonio López Osés half-
title, 41

Bodegas Fariña S.L. 52

Codorníu S.A., Spain 109

Martini & Rossi Limited
101

**Robert Harding Picture
Library Limited** 61, 89

**The Sherry Institute of
Spain** 86/87

Zefa Picture Library
jacket, 121, 126

Contents_____

Page

How to Use this Book   6

Foreword   7

Introduction   8
The System of Classification   10
Motoring in Spain   12
Visiting a Bodega   14

Navarra   16
The Wines of Navarra   18
Pamplona   20
Navarra's Wine Country   21
Food and Festivals   24

The Rioja   26
Rioja – the Bordeaux Legacy   28
Wine Country of the Rioja Baja   30
Logroño   32
Rioja Alta and Alavesa   34
Ollauri and Haro   38
Food and Festivals   40

Aragon   42
Wines and Wine Villages of Aragon   44

Old Castile and Galicia   46
The Wines of Old Castile   48
The Ribera del Duero   50
Valladolid, Tordesillas and Toro   52
Rueda   54
The Mountains of Segovia   56
Food and Festivals   58
Galicia   60

New Castile   62
The Wines of New Castile   64
Madrid, Aranjuez, Toledo   66
La Mancha   68
Valdepeñas   71

Food and Festivals   74

Andalusia   76
Córdoba   78
Montilla   80
Málaga   82
From Málaga to Jerez   85
Sherry Styles   86
Sherry and the Solera System   88
The Sherry Country   90
Food and Festivals   96

Catalonia   98
The Wines of Catalonia   100
The Ampurdán and Alella   102
Barcelona   105
The Penedès and CAVA   106
The Raimat Estate   111
Tarragona   112
The Mountains of Catalonia   113
Food and Festivals   116

The Levante and the Islands   118
The Wines of the Levante   120
Valencia   122
From Valencia to Utiel-Requena   124
Requena to Almansa   125
Villena and Yecla   127
Jumilla and Monóvar   128
Food and Festivals   130
The Islands – Balearics and Canaries   132

Reference Section   133
Glossary of Wine and Food Terms   133
Grape Varieties   135
Spanish Vintages   137
Further Information   138
Further Reading   141

Index   142

How to Use this Book

This book is designed to give as much practical help to the serious wine traveller in Spain as possible. Chapter by chapter, the reader is given an introduction to the different wine regions and cuisines of Spain, and guided through the countryside to its best-known wineries and wine towns, as well as other historic sights, towns and cities. Special advice about driving in Spain and about visiting bodegas can be found on pages 12 to 15; and general tourist information is given on pages 139 to 140. Sources of further information on wines appear on pages 138 and 141. Each chapter has its regional map, showing its chief towns and sites of major wineries, and giving an outline of the road system. Further route maps of smaller areas are provided wherever necessary.

Information panels

Perhaps most essential to the tourist, however, are the information panels that accompany the text as it guides you through the individual regions. These panels will give you a clear idea of the range of bodegas that can be visited, their opening times, their facilities, and additional points of interest (such as architecture or history). The symbols used are shown above right. The panels also include details on wine museums, some recommended wine shops and restaurants, occasional special food markets, and a useful selection of state-run hotels or Paradors.

The bodegas

Although the selection of bodegas is wide, it does not include every Spanish bodega that is open to the public. This book concentrates on those that are worth visiting either because their wines are outstanding or because their wineries are most touristically attractive. If booking is necessary, it is best to contact the bodega well in advance, by letter (a sample letter in Spanish is given in the Reference Section, on page 140) – and then phone within one or two days of your intended visit to confirm the arrangement (advice on how to use the telephone in Spain is provided on page 140). Most bodegas offer a free tasting, but a purchase of wine, however small, will be much appreciated.

Restaurants

Again, the recommended restaurants are a selection, since it is not possible to give details of all the good restaurants in Spain within the scope of this book. Recommendations are made on the grounds of quality alone. Some of them will be expensive, so it is worth checking the menu displayed outside before you enter the premises. Further guidance on restaurants can be found in books recommended on page 141. Booking, incidentally, is usually recommended on Sundays and in the evenings, particularly in the cities.

Wine shops

Wine retailing in Spain is still considerably under-developed, and there are few specialist shops. Those that are listed are highly recommended, not only because of their selection of fine wines but because you can be confident that the wines have been properly handled and cellared. Other non-specialist shops are also worth browsing in, especially for local curiosities, but their storage conditions may not always be ideal.

Information panel symbols	
E	English spoken
TF	tastings are free
TP	tasting must be paid for
WS	wines for sale
t	telephoning (or writing) in advance advisable
T	telephoning (or writing) in advance essential

Foreword

Spain is a country with a centuries-old tradition of wine-making. On numerous occasions, wine has played a special part in the country's history.

Some 1,600,000 hectares of vineyards, distributed throughout the length and breadth of the country, produce a wide range of wines, each with its own special characteristics. Different climatic conditions; soils with different structures, textures and depths; different varieties of grapes; and the technologies used in the production and ageing of the wines; all of these are factors which have made their contribution to wines that are justifiably famous throughout the world.

This great diversity of wines, coupled with the variety of cuisines that can be found in the different regions, is one of the great attractions for the traveller in Spain. Those who make their journey through the country's varied regions, discovering the many reminders of its colourful history as well as the modern face of Spain, will find in its wines a living symbol of a unique civilization and culture.

Maria Isabel Mijares y Garcia-Pelayo
Secretaire General de l'Union Internationale des Oenologues

Introduction _____

I n the past 15 years Spain has made a series of impressive transitions: from military dictatorship to democracy; from a position on the periphery of Europe to E.E.C. membership; from economic stagnation to industrial power. It is not surprising, therefore, that the Spaniards have rediscovered an interest and pride in everything Spanish, their culture, their lifestyles, their fashion and their cuisine.

Yet Spain is still in many respects an unknown country. The millions of tourists who flood its seaside resorts each year hardly venture more than a short way inland. Meanwhile, the great hinterland, with its historic cities, its mighty mountain ranges, rivers and plateaus remains largely untouched.

Luckily the wine regions are mostly in the interior, in unspoilt countryside far from the coastal belt. As a result, a wine tour of Spain has some logistical complications. But it reveals a range of cultural and gastronomic experiences that few tourists on the crowded Costas know exists.

This book outlines two basic routes through Spain's wine regions that lead from north to south. The first begins at the western end of the Pyrenees and leads you through the interior, from Navarra, into the Rioja, then Old and New Castile, ending in the southern region of Andalusia. The second route is simpler, following the Mediterranean coast from the French border southwards to Alicante, passing through Catalonia and the Levante district.

Within each region a special wine route is suggested. And there are two further forays included: one into Galicia from either the Rioja or Old Castile; and another into Aragon from either the Rioja or Catalonia.

The Grand Tour
For the determined traveller a full tour will take some weeks. You can complete one of the north-south tours, either the inland or the coastal route, and then follow the second one in reverse on the return journey. To enjoy this to the full, however, you will need plenty of stamina as well as time.

Shorter visits
If you are planning a shorter visit, there are a number of alternatives. One is a tour covering only the northern regions, travelling through Navarra, the Rioja, Aragon and Catalonia. Or, a longer journey can lead through Navarra, the Rioja, the Castiles, the Levante and Catalonia, ending once again at the French border. But these routes have the disadvantage that they miss out the regions of the South.

Another visit could be dedicated to Andalusia, for this is a large and fascinating province, with enough interest to merit an individual tour. Whichever route you choose, you are likely to be tempted into another. Few tourists can exhaust the attractions in just one trip.

BASQUE PROVINCES

FRANCE

ASTURIAS

R. Miño

● Santiago de Compostela

● Orense

● Pamplona

Logroño ●

Huesca ●

R. Ebro

Barcelona ●

● Valladolid

● Lérida

R. Duero

Zaragoza ●

● Zamora

● Tarragona

● Segovia

● Madrid

PORTUGAL

R. Tagus

● Valencia

● Alcázar de San Juan

EXTREMADURA

R. Jucar

R. Guadiana

● Valdepeñas

R. Segura

● Alicante

MURCIA

R. Guadalquivir

● Córdoba

Seville ●

Málaga ●

● Jerez

	Galicia		Catalonia
	Old Castile		New Castile
	The Rioja		The Levante
	Navarra		Andalusia
	Aragon		The Balearics

The System of Classification

Rioja *The name of the region*

Vino de Crianza
The indication of ageing: a vino de crianza *is a wine in its third year, matured for at least one year in oak cask and a further period in bottle. The* terms reserva, gran reserva *and* cosecha *also indicate the ageing process (see facing page). Strict requirements for ageing are laid down by the* Consejo Regulador

Consejo Regulador de la Denominación de Origen Rioja *The official logo of the Consejo Regulador, which regulates and guarantees the origin of the wine and its quality*

BQ No *The bottling number issued by the Consejo Regulador*

The need for classification

Despite producing less wine than either Italy or France, Spain has more hectares under vine than any other country in the world. Its climate varies considerably from the North, where the influence of the Atlantic predominates, to the regions of the South and East, which are more Mediterranean in character, and the result is a wide variety of types of wines.

Although the progress achieved by Spain's wine industry has been impressive in recent years, it has also been uneven, with the production and ageing facilities of some regions lagging well behind those of others. To hasten improvements the Spanish authorities, encouraged by the E.E.C., have created an official system to guarantee the consumer a minimum level of quality and give him or her some guidance.

A gran reserva *(far left)* is a wine made from a great vintage. It has been aged for at least three years in oak cask and three in bottle. A reserva *(left)* is a selected wine that has been aged for at least three years, of which a minimum of one year must have been in cask. Wines with little or no ageing usually have the word cosecha *(vintage)* followed by a date only. The letters *C.V.C* (Contiene Varias Cosechas) *means that the wine is a blend of several vintages.*

The Denominations of Origin

Central to this system are the *Denominaciónes de Origen* or Denominations of Origin (D.O.s), similar to the French *Appellations Contrôlées* or Italian *Denominazioni d'Origine*. In 1988 there were 30 of these dotted around the country, each overseen by a Consejo Regulador (C.R.) or Regulating Council. As the regions' quality watchdogs, these Consejos oversee virtually every aspect of wine production and ageing: they ensure that the wine is made from grapes grown within the delimited area; that it is made from authorized varieties; and that the wineries in which it is made are suitably equipped and maintain a high standard of cleanliness and hygiene.

Furthermore, every year the Consejos reject any parcel of wine that they do not consider to be of sufficient quality, which is then either sold off in bulk or distilled. These standards are exacting. But every bottle that meets them is then entitled to the coveted label on the back of every D.O. wine.

The back label also gives the consumer an indication of the ageing that the wine has undergone. In general Spanish wines are divided into *vinos del año*, *crianzas*, *reservas* or *gran reservas*, depending on how much ageing they have been given.

There are, of course, some fine wines that are produced outside the D.O. network and which are not entitled to a Consejo back label – the wines of Raimat in Catalonia are a good example. But, most of the time, an official back label is the consumer's best guarantee of reliability and quality.

Motoring in Spain

There are three main points to keep in mind if you are driving in Spain. First, Spain does not have a good safety record. For example, it is estimated that you are six times more likely to be involved in a traffic accident in Spain than in the U.K. This may compare favourably with some other European countries, but it is a sobering statistic. Second, Spanish drink-driving laws, although strict on paper, are lax in practice, and it is still quite common to see roadside cafés at lunchtime packed with lorry drivers drinking wine and brandy. Third, Spain is one of the most mountainous countries in Europe, so driving here can be hazardous.

Obviously, you must always drive with care:

Contrasting landscapes. Varieties planted in the cool northern regions (above) include classic French grapes. The southern vineyards (right) produce the famous fortified wines.

* remember to drive on the right, and give way to traffic from the right.
* seatbelts are compulsory outside town or city boundaries.
* you must have a regulation G.B. sticker on a G.B.-registered car, and carry a breakdown triangle.
* always carry a spare tyre and a jack, and a reserve of oil, water and petrol. (Petrol stations and garages are scarce in remoter regions.)
* make sure you are well insured.
* last but not least, do not get tempted into prolonged lunchtime drinking or tastings if you have to drive afterwards.

The roads

The **nacionales** are the main thoroughfares in Spain and are usually crowded. In particular, they are used by most of the big lorries, which can make for frustrating driving, especially in mountainous areas. The **autopistas** carry comparatively light traffic, as they have tolls, but they make long journeys comfortable, and their service areas are usually excellent. The *autopistas* are a good way to bypass large cities. Lower in rank are the C roads which link towns in rural areas. These are generally narrow and vary in quality from good to appalling (hence the possible need for spare tyres).

Signposts for the *autopistas* are in white letters on a blue ground as opposed to those of the *nacionales* and C roads, which have black letters on a white ground.

SPEED LIMITS
Urban areas 60kph/37mph
Normal roads 90–100kph/ 56–62mph
Motorways 120kph/74mph

Petrol
CAMPSA, the national petrol distribution company, sells three grades:
Standard (gasolina) 90 octane.
Super 96 octane.
Extra 98 octane.

Documents
You should keep your passport and driving licence with you at all times.

Insurance
Consult your local A.A. office or insurance company. To be on the safe side it is worth getting a Green Card and increasing your insurance cover (for yourself and for any passengers). The costs of litigation in Spain are high.

Driving tips
To avoid traffic jams, don't drive in to cities on Sunday nights or out of them on Sunday mornings.

Never leave your car unlocked, and don't leave valuables in view. If possible, use hotel car parks, or guarded ones.

Visiting a Bodega

All hotels are registered with the local authorities and have light-blue square plaques with white lettering at their entrance. The difference between the categories may often be slight but, in ascending order, they are as follows:

F Fonda.
CH Casa de Huespedes.
P Pension.
Hs Hostal. (More expensive, but still cheap by European standards.)
HsH Hostal Residencia. (These are classified by one, two or three stars.)
H Hotel. (These are graded from one star to five.)

Finally, at the top end of the scale (though they are often cheaper than the top hotels) are the state-run Paradores Nacionales. These are usually housed in beautifully restored monuments, such as monasteries or castles. Their prices vary enormously, according to location and time of year.

Bodegas and co-operatives

Amongst the best welcomes in Spain are to be found in Jerez, in the far south corner. As you drive into the town you are greeted by billboards inviting you to visit the sherry bodegas. Most of the leading firms have guided tours of their premises which end with a tasting and usually include a video on sherry production.

But Jerez is the exception rather than the rule. In general the Spanish wine industry has not yet woken up to wine tourism. Comparatively few of its bodegas are prepared to give tours of their premises (though membership of a wine club or a wine appreciation circle will certainly help you), and many do not even sell wine on the premises.

Unfortunately, this means that you will not find an automatic welcome from all of the companies which rate a mention in this book. Their wines, however, will almost always be available in local restaurants and wine shops.

Fortunately, the co-operatives are usually hospitable. They may not be the most exciting wineries, but they are mainly more than willing to give tastings and to sell wine to the passer-by. Once you are on their premises, it may be fairly easy to persuade them to conduct a short tour.

Booking ahead

Those other companies that are open to the public are listed with relevant information in the data panels in

Different regions of Spain have their traditional styles of bodega architecture. The cellars of Domecq's bodegas in Jerez, for example, are distinctly Andalusian in character. Their vaulted cellars with horse-shoe arches are built along the lines of Córdoba's famous mosque, the Mezquita (see page 79).

each section, along with recommended wine shops and restaurants. In most cases it is necessary to book in advance. If you decide to do this by letter, you should leave plenty of time for a reply. An extended trip around the wine regions of Spain needs and deserves this careful planning.

These visits are nearly always well worth the extra effort. The Spanish are very hospitable, and if you have taken the trouble to write or telephone in advance you will be greeted with characteristic courtesy.

So, if you make an appointment, do be sure to honour it. And, if you are delayed along the way, do telephone your hosts if you can (see the section on using the telephone in Spain, and a sample letter, on pages 140–141).

There is an added bonus to most bodega visits. There are many styles of winery – for example, the bodegas of Andalusia are very different from those of Catalonia. And, while some companies have made great efforts to keep up with modern viniculture, others maintain an unshakeable loyalty to tradition.

In contrast to the traditional bodega architecture of Andalusia, the wineries of Catalonia are often highly modernized, making full use of advanced technology. The stainless steel fermentation tanks shown above belong to the Codorníu winery in San Sadurní de Noya.

Navarra

To get to Pamplona
Pamplona is 160km (100 miles) south of Bilbao along the A68 (tolls), the N1 and the N240 (no tolls) and the A15 (tolls); it is 80km (50 miles) north of Logroño along the N111 (no tolls); 430km (270 miles) north-east of Madrid along the N1 to Burgos, the N120 to Logroño and the N111 (no tolls); or 480km (300 miles) via the N1 to Burgos, the A1 and A68 (tolls), and the N111 (no tolls).

Navarra, as the traveller will soon discover, is a region that is steeped in history. From the moment that you cross the border, preferably through the historic Pyrenean pass of Roncesvalles made famous by the *Song of Roland*, you become aware of an active, restless and war-torn past. Navarra was formerly a proud, independent kingdom which reached the zenith of its power in the 11th century, when it stretched to Bordeaux in the North and Barcelona in the East. It has witnessed, and suffered, a constant ebb and flow of conquering or retreating armies from the time of the Moors, forced southward by Charlemagne, to the Civil War, when Carlist volunteers rallied in their thousands to the Nationalist cause. On a more peaceful note, the northern part of the province is crossed by the route to Santiago de Compostela, and its numerous chapels and churches are a testimony to the pilgrims.

Today Navarra is a prosperous province producing excellent meat and vegetables as well as wine. Its countryside has often been described as a microcosm of Spain with the Pyrenean hills of the North giving way to the flat, dry plains of the South.

A trout-filled river flows through the small town of Sumbilla in the Pyrenean north of Navarra.

The point of departure for the wine traveller is the ancient and historic city of Pamplona, which can be reached from France by one of two routes. You can drive along the C133 which becomes the N121 and branches off from the A1 *autopista* (the continuation of the French A63) at the border. Devotees of history may wish to follow the more rugged Pyrenean C135 which begins at the mountain pass of Roncesvalles close to the French towns of Valcarlos and St Jean-Pied-de-Port.

If you hire a car at Bilbao you will have to circle the city on the motorway ring roads and leave on the A68 *autopista* which rises to the high Puerto de Altube. Then take the turning to Vitoria and follow the well-signposted N1 and N240. Those arriving on the Santander ferry should take the route to Bilbao and then follow the same instructions.

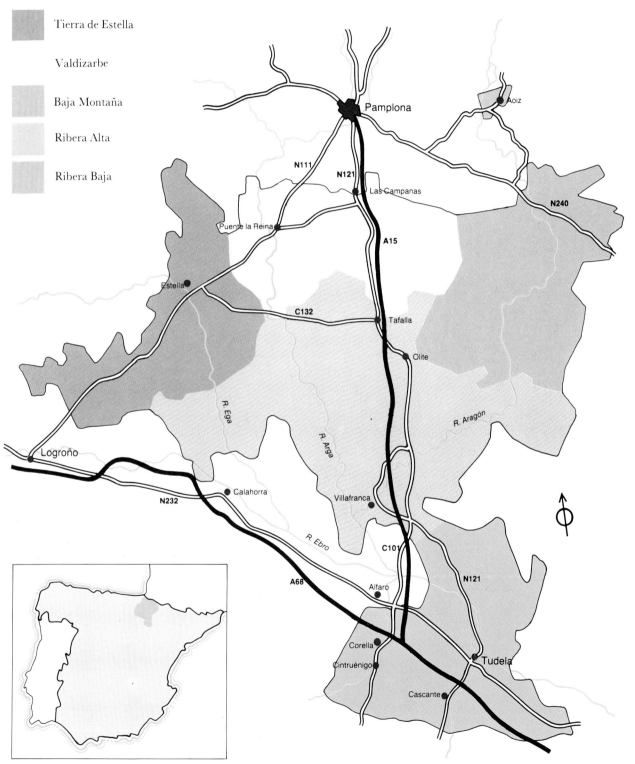

Tierra de Estella

Valdizarbe

Baja Montaña

Ribera Alta

Ribera Baja

Pamplona

Aoiz

N111

N121

Las Campanas

N240

Puente la Reina

A15

Estella

C132

Tafalla

Olite

R. Ega

R. Arga

R. Aragón

Logroño

Calahorra

Villafranca

N232

R. Ebro

C101

N121

A68

Alfaro

Corella

Tudela

Cintruénigo

Cascante

The Wines of Navarra

The Denomination of Origin of Navarra covers some 19,000 hectares of vineyards between Pamplona and the great Ebro river. It is divided into five sub-regions: the Valdizarbe around Puente la Reina; the Baja Montaña on the border with Aragon to the east; the Tierra Estella around the town of Estella; the Ribera Alta around Olite; and the Ribera Baja around Cintruénigo and Tudela. The altitude drops as you move south leading to higher temperatures and lower rainfall. The region produces about 563,000 hectolitres of wine a year with a guarantee of origin.

'The Rioja for reds, the Penedès for whites and Navarra for *rosados*' goes an old Spanish saying. It is somewhat outdated now and infuriates producers from all three regions, but it does highlight the great strength of the Navarra wine industry. For although the region has produced prestigious reds for many years, it is undoubtedly the quality of its *rosados* that has enabled Navarra to establish itself as one of Spain's leading quality wine producers.

The great *rosados*

But what is the basis of this quality? The answer is undoubtedly the character of the much-maligned but frequently planted Garnacha grape, which thrives in the region's climate. When picked early and macerated for only a short time to extract just the right amount of colour from the skin, there can be little doubt that it produces some of the very best rosés in Spain – dark pink in colour, fruity and lightish in alcohol (12–13 per cent). More importantly, they are dry, very much drier than those made in other parts of Europe, with

more body, structure and complexity. Those that are aged in wood have interesting brick-yellow colour overtones and a subtle touch of oak.

It is a very great pity that these wines are not better known and more widely appreciated abroad. In Spain, they are very popular. So much so that, while in the early 1970s they only accounted for about 25 per cent of the region's production, by 1985, encouraged by enthusiastic domestic demand, this percentage had increased to over half.

A change of focus

In more recent years, however, the region's producers have focused their attention on improving the quality of their reds and whites. Both Spain's entry into the European Community and the phenomenal success of Rioja in foreign markets have persuaded them to adapt and expand their range of wines to meet the exacting standards of the international marketplace. The result has been an impressive level of investment in the region's wineries

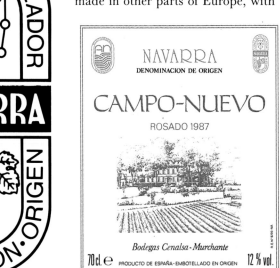

Much of the winery of Vinícola Navarra in Las Campanas dates back to 1850. The company is now a leading wine producer in the region. The recent installations of high-technology equipment here contrast with the old bodegas (see page 21).

and vineyards, which has been encouraged and supported by the provincial government.

The new wineries

The most dramatic progress has been achieved in the improvement of the region's production and ageing centres. Even the co-operatives, which account for most of the region's production and are not usually regarded as a progressive force, have invested heavily in their facilities. All over the region lighter crushers, stainless steel fermentation tanks and oak barrels for ageing are being installed.

New vineyards

Progress in the region's vineyards has been slower and less dramatic but impressive nevertheless. Today, any farmer willing to replant his vineyard more efficiently and with varieties approved by the Consejo (see pages 10–11), qualifies for the cheap loans available from the Government. Planting of Tempranillo, Viura and even Chardonnay and Cabernet Sauvignon, is therefore increasing.

Improving wines

The result of these developments is that the quality of Navarra's reds and whites has improved immensely in recent years. Greater use of Viura, together with cold fermentation equipment to help preserve the wines' elusive aromas, has increased the production of crisp, fruity whites.

Better vinification and the earlier picking of the grapes to increase acidity and to lower the alcohol content has enabled the producers to make young reds from the Garnacha that have better balance and fruit. More Tempranillo, which can cope better with the rigours of wood ageing than the Garnacha, has led to increased production of finer and longer-lived *crianzas* and *reservas*.

Together with the great *rosados*, these wines already make up a wide range. When more replanted vineyards have come to maturity, particularly those with 'noble' varieties that will add an extra dimension, the region's wines will improve further. Navarra is clearly a region to watch.

Grape varieties

Despite recent progress, the Garnacha is still Navarra's leading grape variety covering some 85 per cent of the entire vineyard area. There are, however, increased plantings of other varieties, especially Tempranillo, Cabernet Sauvignon and Viura on the higher ground of the Tierra Estella and the Ribera Alta.

Pamplona

PAMPLONA
Recommended wine shops:
Casa Chavez Sancho el Fuerte 8, Pamplona. Wide selection from all regions of Spain.
Museo del Vino Sancho el Fuerte 77, Pamplona. Wide selection from all regions of Spain.

Recommended restaurants:
Josetxo Estafeta 73, Pamplona. Tel: 22 20 97. Sophisticated Navarran food.
Las Pocholas Paseo de Saraste 6, Pamplona. Tel: 21 17 29. Traditional Navarran food.

Pamplona, as any reader of Hemingway will tell you, is best known in Spain for the Feria de San Fermin, the famous bullfighting fiesta in July.

Behind this flamboyant reputation, however, lies a pulsating regional capital with a compact centre of narrow streets flanked by tall, old houses and more open modern districts of wide avenues. It has an interesting Gothic cathedral, lovely gardens and a massive central fort, the *Ciudadela*.

Eating and drinking
Pamplona is neither a gastronomic nor a wine centre, and has no bodegas. Its chief attraction to the wine traveller is that, in its restaurants, bars and shops, you can find the greatest range of regional wines available. The city gives the visitor an opportunity to become acquainted with the wines and cuisine of the region before embarking on a tour

Two good restaurants are listed here (left), but those looking for local colour are recommended to stroll the streets of the centre and, after an apéritif, to eat in one of the city's unpretentious *asadores*. These are roasting houses where enormous portions of meat are grilled on an open fire and served with salad or other vegetables.

If you ask for the house wine it will be served in an earthenware jar and will be rough and ready. The wines of the leading firms in the region will, however, also be represented on the wine list. The bigger restaurants usually offer a greater selection, which will not be restricted to the wines of the region.

The city has several good hotels in the centre. Parking can be difficult despite the large car park near the Avenida del Ejército.

The bust of the American author Ernest Hemingway, commemorating his frequent visits to the Feria de San Fermin, stands outside the bullring in Pamplona.

Navarra's Wine Country

The wine country of Navarra begins immediately to the South of Pamplona. It is best to leave the city on the busy N121 in the direction of Tudela, the province's second city. First stop is at the town of Las Campanas some 15km (9 miles) from Pamplona, the home of Vinícola Navarra, which stands on the left-hand side of the road. This company has recently gone through a period of lavish investment to modernize its wine-making equipment, but the older part of the winery dates back to 1850 and has been carefully restored. In a way, the company symbolizes Navarra itself, with its traditions and new developments.

Puente la Reina

Just on the other side of the town a turning to the West will lead you through hilly country dotted with vineyards and asparagus to Puente la Reina. This was the junction of the pilgrim routes which entered Spain through the passes of Somport and Roncesvalles, and there is a statue of a pilgrim at the entrance to the town.

The huge Señorio de Sarria, a mixed farm complete with workers' village, and the producer of what are often regarded as the region's finest wines, lies on the outskirts. Guided tours are organized for large groups, otherwise it remains firmly shut.

LAS CAMPANAS
Vinícola Navarra Las Campanas. Tel: 36 01 31 (Manuel Mújico). Mon-Fri 0800–1300, 1500–1800. Closed 1–15 Aug. TF. WS. E. T. Housed in 19th–century buildings.

The 16th-century fortress of the kings of Navarra, with its 15 towers, dominates the unofficial capital of the Navarra wine country, the town of Olite. Ochoa wines illustrate the fortress on their labels (see facing page).

ESTELLA
Bodegas Irache Ayegui, Estella. Tel: 55 19 32 (Javier Garcia). Mon-Fri 1000–1300, 1500–1900, Sat 1000–1300. TF. WS. T. Wine museum.

CORELLA
Bodegas Camilo Castilla S.A. Clle Santa Barbara, Corella. Tel: 78 00 06/ 78 10 21 (Fernando Ferrer or Sñrta Anna Beltrán). Mon-Fri 0800–1300, 1500–1800. TF. WS. T. Collection of agricultural tools. Old oak barrels and vats.

TAFALLA
Recommended restaurant:
Hostal Tafalla, Ctra Pamplona-Zaragoza Km 38, Tafalla. Tel: 870 03 00. Sophisticated Navarran food.

Puente la Reina has witnessed the tramp of countless pilgrims over the hump-backed bridge that crosses the Arga river.

Estella
A few kilometres to the South of Puente la Reina on the N111 you come to Estella, also on the pilgrim route to Santiago. The fascinating architecture of this small town, built on both banks of the Ega river, includes the old palace of the Kings of Navarra. In the 19th century the palace became the headquarters of the Carlists, the supporters of Don Carlos de Borbón, Pretender to the Spanish throne.

Across the river, in the neighbouring hamlet of Ayegui, is the monastery of Irache, another stop on the pilgrim route. In the 16th century the monastery became a Benedictine university. Next door is the winery of Bodegas Irache, one of the region's leading wine companies, which is particularly well known for its red *crianzas* and *reservas*.

Tafalla and Olite
From Ayegui it is necessary to double back along the N111 for a short way and then to take the small and rugged C132 that leads you to Tafalla. This is a small, rather dull town, but close to the exit from the *autopista* is the Hostal Tafalla which has one of the best restaurants of the region.

Unless you are stopping for lunch, it is best to continue along the N121 to Olite, with its oenological station (centre of the region's wine studies), the unofficial capital of Navarra's wine industry. The town is over-shadowed by its great fortress, with its massive ramparts and 15 towers, originally built in the 16th century by

Charles the Noble. Part of this monument has now been refurbished into a comfortable Parador Nacional which makes an ideal overnight stop. There are two small but prestigious wine companies, Bodegas Ochoa and Bodegas Carricas, both in the centre of the old town.

Corella

From Olite, it is a long drive down to the southern part of the wine country. There are two routes, the N121 and the more comfortable A15.

As you drive southwards, the mountainous scenery of the North gives way to the flat plains that characterize the South of Navarra, and the Rioja. Here the Denominations of Navarra and the Rioja lie on the banks of the Ebro river. The wine towns, Cintruénigo and Corella in Navarra and Alfaro and San Adrián in the Rioja, are similar in character; hot in the summer, dusty and quiet.

Of the two in Navarra, Corella, which is built on a hill, is the more attractive although there are few special points of interest for the tourist. Beside the C123 on the outskirts is the winery of Bodegas Bardón, one of the new breed of modern Navarra wine companies which produces good young wines.

In the town itself, the older Hermanos Camilo Castilla has an attractive winery dating back to the last century with row upon row of ancient oak barrels. This is a company with a difference, for although it does produce table wines, its real speciality is the sweet Moscatel dessert wine. The perfume released by this aromatic wine seems to have permeated every wall and beam of this venerable old company.

Cintruénigo

From Corella, it is no more than a short hop to Cintruénigo, a town that is dominated by Bodegas Julián Chivite, the largest of Navarra's wine firms. It is also one of the most prestigious, and the bodega itself, with its oak barrels, cooperage and modern equipment is a testimony to the commitment of three generations of the Chivite family to the production of fine wine.

Further travel

Cintruénigo is a mere 20-minute drive from Alfaro, the first town in the Rioja Baja. Alternatively, the N232 leads to the Denomination of Campo de Borja in Aragon.

CINTRUENIGO
Bodegas Julián Chivite
Clle Ribera s/n, Cintruénigo, Navarra. Tel: 81 10 00 (Sñrta Mercedes Chivite). Mon-Fri 1000–1400, 1600–1800. TF. E. T. Wine for sale at a nearby shop.

MUNCHANTE
Bodegas CENALSA Ctra Tudela, Munchante. Tel: 22 72 83 (Miguel Merino). Mon-Fri 0900–1400, 1530–1730. Closed Aug. TP. T. The winery is not open to the public but its wines can be tasted and bought (by the case) on the premises.

OLITE
Bodegas Ochoa S.A. Ctra Zaragoza 21, 31390 Olite. Tel: 74 00 06. Mon- Fri 0900–1300, 1600–1800. Closed 12–25 Sep. TF. This company is not open to the public, but its wines can be tasted and bought on the premises.

Recommended hotel:
Parador Nacional 'Principe de Viana', Plaza de San Francisco, Olite. Tel: 70 05 00.

At Julián Chivite's winery at Cintruénigo, fermentation takes place in temperature controlled stainless steel tanks.

Food and Festivals

FOOD SPECIALITIES

Bacalao al Ajoarriero There are many very sophisticated variations to this traditional dish. It comes from the northern part of the region and used to be served to *arrieros* (muleteers) at roadside inns in the evening. The traditional version combines salt cod from the Basque coast with garlic, peppers and sometimes tomatoes and onions. In leading restaurants, prawns, crayfish and even lobster are added.

Truchas a la Navarra Fried trout, often stuffed with ham and served with mushrooms, garlic and parsley.

Caldereta Ribereña As this is a peasant dish from the South of the province, the ingredients tend to vary. Basically, it is a stew made with whatever the cook has to hand.

Cordero en Chilindrón Although roast lamb is as popular in Navarra as it is throughout northern Spain, this is a typical and delicious alternative. The lamb is cooked with slices of ham and a sauce of garlic, onions, tomatoes and, of course, the famous red peppers. A variation is *Pimientos en Chilindrón* with large slices of peppers used instead of the lamb.

Perdices a la Tudelana As its name implies, this is a dish from the southern part of the province. Partridges are cooked with quartered apples and served with boiled potatoes and mushrooms.

Festoons of chorizo *sausages, a speciality of Navarra, hang in the shops and market stalls of Navarran towns along with the black* morcilla *sausage, often richly flavoured with cinnamon, pine nuts and raisins.*

FESTIVALS

Curiously, Navarra has no big wine fair. Virtually every town in the wine country celebrates the end of the *vendimia* (the grape harvest) in September or October, but here there is nothing to compare to San Mateo in Logroño or the *'Feria de la Vendimia'* in Jerez.

Despite this, Navarra has a fiesta which is like no other. Every year from 6–14 July, Pamplona takes a break and explodes into an almost unbelievable week of 'running the bulls', drinking, eating and dancing to celebrate the feast of the city's patron saint. However politicized and commercial 'San Fermín' has become, there can be little doubt that it remains one of the greatest and most exhilarating fiestas in Europe if not in the world. If you want to take part, make sure that you book your hotel room well in advance.

NAVARRA'S CUISINE

Many of the great dishes of Navarra
are also typical of Rioja and Aragon.
Menestra de Verduras and the *chilindrón*
sauce, for example, can be found in
all three regions. In fact the three
provinces are interrelated in many
ways, historically and culturally, and
it is not surprising that their regional
cuisines bear a family likeness. But in
general, perhaps because of its more
varied climate, it is Navarra that
offers the greatest diversity.

Mushrooms, trout and game

The province's cooks have an
excellent range of local ingredients at
their disposal. Wild mushrooms grow
in abundance, mostly in the North,
and their sublime flavour can best be
appreciated in the famous *Revuelto de
setas*, where they are combined with
beaten eggs and garlic. The North
also produces from its mountain
streams a wealth of trout, which are
the centrepiece of the province's most
famous dish, *Truchas a la Navarra*.
There are also small game birds,
particularly quail (*codornices*) and
partridges (*perdices*), prepared in a
variety of ways, with vegetables,
wine and even with bitter chocolate.

Artichokes, asparagus, peppers

The southern part of the province,
and particularly the Ribera region
on the banks of the Ebro, is famous
for its vegetables, and vegetable
patches are often a feature of the
landscape, especially the bright
green clumps of asparagus fern.

The artichokes and asparagus from
the region are delicious. They are
usually served as entrées with either
mayonnaise or vinaigrette.

This area is also the home of what

are generally regarded as the best
red peppers of the country, the
pimientos del pico, so-called because of
their beak-shaped ends. These are
usually fried, to accompany grilled
meat, or stuffed with a variety of
different ingredients, or made into
the famous *chilindrón* sauce which
accompanies two other very typical
Navarra dishes, the *Cordero* (roast
lamb) or the *Pimientos en Chilindrón*
(see facing page).

*A visit to the covered market in
Pamplona will reveal an
excellent display of local
products, ranging from fish and
game to the region's vegetables.*

The Rioja

With its powerful agricultural base, the Rioja is one of the richest provinces of Spain, producing some of the finest vegetables in the country as well as famous wines. Its wine production may be small when compared to that of other regions such as La Mancha or Valencia, but it still remains Spain's premier table-wine producer.

This is also a congenial region to visit since eating and drinking are taken seriously and the hospitality of the people is legendary. The landscape offers a contrast between the flat plains of the Rioja Baja and the more rugged terrain of the Alta and Alavesa, both of which are overshadowed by the brooding mountains of the Sierra de Cantabria.

Rioja – the grapes

With vineyards in three provinces – the Rioja itself, Navarra and the Alava – the demarcated wine region of the Rioja is divided into three zones: the Rioja Baja, to the South and East; the Rioja Alavesa to the North of the Ebro; and the Rioja Alta to the West of Logroño.

Because of different soils and climates and the predominance of different grape varieties, these three sub-regions produce red wines that are very different in style: the Baja, where the Garnacha predominates, tends to produce open, fruity wines with good colour and high in alcohol. The Alta and the Alavesa, where the Tempranillo is king, produce leaner, less luscious wines but with greater aroma, elegance and acidity to help them improve during long periods of barrel ageing.

Although there are some wines produced using grapes from only one sub-region, usually the Alta or the Alavesa, most Riojas are blends of wines from the three zones.

The route

Because the N232 and the A68 flow through the region from south-east to north-west, like vital arteries, the wine route is comparatively straightforward.

The Rioja Baja

From Cintruénigo and Corella, where the tour of Navarra ends, it is a short drive along local roads to Alfaro, the first wine town of the Rioja Baja (or Low Rioja). From there it is about 20km (12 miles) to the larger town of Calahorra where detours can be taken to Arnedo or San Adrián. From there you can approach Logroño, the region's capital, via the N232 or the A68.

The Rioja Alavesa

Fuenmayor, the first wine town of the Rioja Alta (or High Rioja) is a mere 10km (6 miles) further up the N232. Here a small country road leads northward into the Rioja Alavesa and the town of Laguardia with its two wineries at the foot of the Sierra de Cantabria. You then drive down again along a similar road to the town of Elciego, the birthplace of the modern Riojan wine industry.

The Rioja Alta

From Elciego it is another short but scenic hop down the N232 and Cenicero, our second town in the Alta, and then another 30km (19 miles) to Haro, with an interesting detour to Paternina cellars at the hamlet of Ollauri on the way.

The Iregua river valley is typical of the rugged terrain of the Rioja Alta.

To get to Logroño
Logroño is 130km (88miles) S of Bilbao on the A68; 350km (217miles) NE of Madrid on the N1 to Burgos, then the N120 (no tolls), or 400km (250miles) via the N1 to Burgos, and the A1 and A68 (tolls).

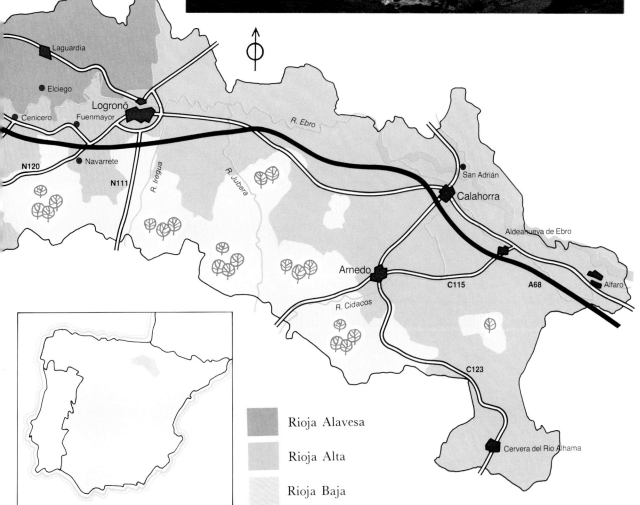

Rioja Alavesa

Rioja Alta

Rioja Baja

Rioja – the Bordeaux Legacy

The Denominación de Origen Rioja covers 47,018 hectares of vineyards, which is about 2.2 per cent of Spain's vineyard area. Its annual production varies, usually between 120 and 140 million litres, about 3 per cent of the country's total wine production.

IMPERIAL
RESERVA
1978
Rioja

Compañía Vinícola
del Norte de España, s.a.

13% Vol.   HARO LA RIOJA
75 cl. e

PRODUCE OF SPAIN

Harvesting Tempranillo grapes in the Rioja Alta.

It often comes as a surprise to discover the extent of the Rioja's debt to Bordeaux. For it is this great French region that has been chiefly responsible, however indirectly, for the two boom periods that created the Riojan industry as it exists today.

Up to the middle of the last century the Rioja made wine in a similar way to other Spanish regions, crushing the grapes and fermenting their juice in open stone *lagars*.

Then, in the 1860s, the phylloxera, a louse that attacks the vine and destroys its roots, laid waste the vineyards of France forcing the wine brokers or *négociants* to seek other sources of supply. In the Rioja they found a region with enormous potential, opened up buying offices and brought with them their technicians and wine-makers.

Oak vats and barrels

The phylloxera eventually spread to Spain but by then the Rioja had grown and many of the methods of ageing and production introduced by the French had taken firm root.

Bordeaux's greatest legacy was the use of oak. The wines were fermented in huge oak vats and, after a period of rest, were pumped into the classic Bordelais barrel of 225 litres where they were aged for several years. It is this period of oak ageing that is chiefly responsible for the distinctive character of traditional Riojas. The whites deepen to an almost golden colour and achieve a unique concentration of fruit, flavour and acidity. The reds on the other hand lighten to a dark tawny colour with a wonderful balance between fruit and oakiness. All have the distinctive soft vanilla flavour that is the region's hallmark.

The boom of the 1970s

Not all the region's wines are made in this way, however. For, in the 1970s, the Rioja experienced another revolution that was as far reaching as the one of the 19th century. Again, Bordeaux acted as a catalyst.

In the first years of the decade, claret prices exploded and wine traders once more had to look to other regions. They soon rediscovered the Rioja where wine was still being made in the way it had been in Bordeaux before the phylloxera. From relative obscurity, the region was dragged into the international limelight. Demand triggered off an immense flow of investment. It also brought in new personnel, wine-makers and marketing men, who knew what was

drunk and how wine was made in other countries. Their influence was quickly felt.

The new wines

The greatest change introduced was in the production of whites and rosés. The 'modernists' began to ferment them at low temperatures to preserve their aroma and freshness. They also began to release the wines younger.

The change in the red wines was more subtle. Instead of ageing them for long periods in barrel, bottling and releasing them six months later, they began to age the wines for less time in barrel and for longer in bottle. The result is that they are less oaky, but perhaps more complex and elegant.

The original oak fermentation vats at Marqués de Riscal installed by the French technician Jean Pineau.

The Tempranillo is the leading red grape variety of the region, covering some 42 per cent of the entire vineyard area. It is followed by the Garnacha which covers about 32 per cent and lesser quantities of Graciano and Mazuelo, usually planted in small parcels in the Alta.

White wines are usually made from the Viura but the Malvasía and the Garnacha Blanca are also permitted.

Wine Country of the Rioja

*The tree-lined central square in the old Roman
city of Calahorra, in the Rioja Baja, is famous
for a notorious casino, where whole estates are
said to have been gambled away.*

Following the suggested route (see
page 26), the tour begins in the Rioja
Baja, the warmest and lowest of the
region's three sub-zones, a flat plain
of ochre-coloured fields lying
alongside the great Ebro river. As
few bodegas are based here, it is not
an area often visited by wine buffs.
But there are quiet, pleasant towns,
and there is plenty to entertain the
palate (like neighbouring Ribera, it is
well known for early vegetables).

The Garnacha dominates the
extensive vineyards, producing
wines with colour, body and a
comparatively high level of alcohol.

Alfaro

From Cintruénigo, where the tour of
Navarra ended, it is a small step
across the regional border to Alfaro.
This is a small agricultural town and
the home of one of the Rioja's most
up-and-coming wine companies,
Bodegas Palacio Remondo, still
family-owned and run. The winery,
a combination of modern equipment
and old buildings, is next door to the
Hotel Palacios owned by the same
family. As it has a wine museum, a
small museum of fossils and various
antiquities, a congenial café well
patronized by local agricultural
workers as well as a more
sophisticated restaurant, it is a good
place to stay. Nearby is also one of
the best restaurants of the Baja, the
Asador San Roque, which offers

well-prepared regional food with excellent vegetable dishes.

Calahorra
The alternative is to continue up the N232 to the pleasant old Roman city of Calahorra. This is one of the largest towns of the Rioja, a commercial centre serving the local agricultural community. Calahorra has several good restaurants as well as one of the region's two Paradors.

Arnedo and San Adrián
Calahorra is not a wine town, however. If it is bodegas that you are after, there are two routes to follow. Either go southwards along small, difficult side roads to Arnedo where Bodegas Faustino Ulecia has its deep, musty cellars carved into the rock. Or drive northwards across the Ebro to the larger and more charming town of San Adrián which,

although in the province of Navarra, is within the delimited area of the Rioja.

Here there are two wineries. The Gurpegui family, who also have cellars in Haro, have a large bottling and warehousing complex in the town for both Rioja and non-denominated wine. Bodegas Muerza, which produces excellent wines, is also close to the centre.

The road to Logroño
From Calahorra it is about 50km (30 miles) to Logroño either along the N232 *nacional* or the more expensive A68 *autopista*. Both of these roads go through the heart of the region to Haro and the Basque country beyond. But the N232 is a busy road, with heavy lorries grinding their way north while the A68 carries very little traffic and is an easy drive, with an exit immediately south of Logroño.

SAN ADRIAN
Bodegas Muerza pl de Vera Magallón I, San Adrián. Tel: 22 72 83 (Miguel Merino). Mon-Fri 0830–1330, 1600–1800. Closed Aug. TF. T. Wines can be tasted and bought (by the case) on the premises.

The Rioja Baja is the warmest, driest and flattest of the three Rioja wine sub-zones. The Garnacha grape thrives here, producing wines strong in alcohol and fruit.

Logroño

The statue of General Espartero in Logroño's central square.

LOGRONO
Bodegas Campo Viejo
Polígono de Cascajos, Clle
Gustavo Becquer 3,
Logroño. Tel: 23 80 00.
Mon-Fri 0800–1300, 1500–
1800. Closed Jul and Aug.
TF. WS. E. T.
**Bodegas Marqués de
Murrietta** Finca YGAY,
Ctra de Zaragoza Km 403,
Logroño. Tel: 25 81 00
(Alfonso Troya). Mon-Fri
0900–1300, and 1500–1900
(in summer, 0700–1500).
Closed Aug. TF. WS. E. T.

Despite its great prosperity, Logroño
is a relatively quiet provincial city.
It can be busy enough though,
particularly on Saturday nights
when the student population throngs
the *tapas* bars (for explanation see
page 96) of the Calle de los Laureles
near the central square, and in
general the bars and restaurants are
overflowing. But the ostentatious
display of wealth which you find in
Spain's other rich cities is missing.
The Riojano is certainly no miser and
he likes to eat and drink, but,
perhaps because he is still essentially
a countryman, he keeps his money
safely in the bank.

Logroño is a real wine city.
Famous labels stare out at you from
bottles in the windows of grocery and
wine shops, while the wine lists of
the restaurants seem to burst with
local pride, displaying what almost
amounts to a roll of honour of the
Spanish wine industry.

The old bodegas . . .
The city is also the home of several
leading bodegas. Some 3km (2
miles) from the city centre, on the
south-bound N232, is the famous
Bodegas Marqués de Murrietta.
Founded in 1848, it claims to be the
oldest existing wine company in the

Rioja. It is now owned by a count from Galicia who has continued the firm's aristocratic lineage. The entrance to the winery is tricky as it can only be approached from the southbound *nacional* and is badly signposted. But, for lovers of wine history, a visit, which has to be arranged in advance, is a must.

Closer to the city centre, on the western bank of the river, is another historic company, Bodegas Franco-Españolas, founded in 1901 by a Frenchman fleeing from phylloxera. Again, the whole complex, with its extensive underground cellars, is lovingly maintained.

. . . and the new

The city's other two bodegas are very different. Both were built during the boom of the 1970s and so represent the modern side of the Rioja coin. The giant Bodegas Campo Viejo, near the city's railway station, is owned by Savin, Spain's largest wine company. It is impressive rather than beautiful with row upon row of oak barrels in long subterranean passageways, and is worth visiting if only to appreciate the size and wealth of parts of the Riojan wine industry.

Finally, buried in an industrial estate on the outskirts of the city, is Bodegas Olarra. This is one of the most surprising wine companies in Spain, for it was built by a steel magnate from Bilbao and has been modelled on the wineries of California. The main building is in the shape of a Y to represent the region's three sub-zones, and the whole complex has a rather Oriental feeling with its pagoda-shaped turrets. It produces a wide range of wines and is one of the most respected companies of the region.

Bodegas Olarra Polígono de Cantabria, Logroño. Tel: 23 52 99 (Marsan Fria). Mon-Fri 0900–1300, and 1500–1900. Closed Aug. TF. WS. E. T. Only open to members of wine clubs or wine appreciation circles.

Recommended wine shops:
Palacio del Vino Av de Burgos 136, Logroño. **Unión Licorera**, Clle Huesca 16, Logroño.

Recommended restaurant:
La Merced Clle Marqués de San Nicolas 136, Logroño. '*Haute cuisine*'. Expensive.

Bodegas Franco-Españolas in Logroño represents Rioja's union of French and Spanish wine-making traditions.

Rioja Alta and Alavesa

If the N232 *nacional* is busy to the East of Logroño, it is even more so to the West. Unfortunately, unless you want to go straight to Haro and miss out on the towns in between, there is no good alternative, as continually joining and leaving the A68 *autopista* is very complicated. Furthermore, the N232 is undoubtedly the best way to see the countryside of the Rioja Alta and Alavesa, with glimpses of vineyards and good views of the river and the Sierra beyond. Once you get off the *nacionales* on to the small C roads, there is relatively little traffic, but the road surfaces often leave a lot to be desired.

Fuenmayor
The N232 leaves Logroño from the south-west and it is no more than 20 to 30 minutes to Fuenmayor, the first of the Alta's wine towns. The centre of the town is dominated by the church and the Casa Real, a crumbling stately home. All around the central square are bars which, at the start of the harvest, the *vendimia*, are packed with itinerant workers waiting for the picking to begin. As in Logroño, Saturday night suddenly transforms the town, even in the winter, when these bars fill up with cheerful grape farmers and wine-makers coming into town for a glass of wine or two.

Fuenmayor is also the home of one the region's largest wine companies, AGE Bodegas Unidas. Made famous by its Siglo Saco brand, clad distinctively in a hessian bag, the firm was formed by the fusion of three old family companies. The impression it

Vineyards line the banks of the River Oja in the Rioja Alta. Here the vines are trained along wires, an unusual sight in Spain, where they are mainly grown as bushes.

gives, however, is one of complete modernity, with up-to-date equipment, open plan offices and well-equipped quality control laboratories. As with Logroño's Campo Viejo, you cannot help but be impressed.

Navarrete

On the outskirts of Navarrete, a small town just on the other side of the A68, are two very different firms, Bodegas Corral and Bodegas Montecillo. Both wineries were built in 1974 following the traditional style of architecture, and are fitted with modern equipment. But while the first is family-owned and prides itself on being one of the few firms entirely in Riojan hands, the second is part of the giant Osborne Group, famous for its sherries and brandies. Both firms are amongst the most prestigious in the region.

Laguardia

The next wine town up the N232 from Fuenmayor is Cenicero, but at this stage it is more fun to make a detour and head northwards to the small town of Laguardia at the foot of the Sierra Cantabrica. Just outside Fuenmayor you cross the provincial border and, despite still being in the delimited zone of the Rioja, you enter the Basque country and the province of Alava. This is the heart of the Rioja Alavesa where the Tempranillo is king and, to the discerning palate, the wine produced is different, warmer, more luscious and richer than the more austere and elegant wines of the Alta.

Laguardia can boast of two bodegas, Bodegas Alavesas founded in the 1970s, and Bodegas Palacio originally founded a century before

Wine is still bottled by hand at the López de Heredia winery in Haro (see page 39). This company remains loyal to traditional wine-making skills.

and now belonging to the Seagram Group of North America. The two wineries stand close to each other against the backdrop of the Sierra, a wonderful sight on a clear, crisp day.

Elciego and Marqués de Riscal

From Laguardia, another small road leads down from the Sierra to the lovely town of Elciego.

For the wine historian, this is a place of pilgrimage as it contains the famous and historic winery of Marqués de Riscal. This was the first winery in the region to be built along French lines by the technician Jean Pineau in 1868. Just to show how close the Rioja came to missing its modern fame and reputation, it is worth briefly recounting the story of this influential Frenchman.

ELCIEGO
Vinos de los Herederos del Marqués de Riscal
Clle Torrea 1, 01340 Elciego. Tel: 10 60 00 (Francisco Hurtado). Mon-Fri 0800–1600. Closed Aug. TF. WS. T.

NAVARRETE
Bodegas Corral Ctra de Logroño Km 10, Navarrete. Tel: 44 01 93 (Sñr Martinez). Mon-Fri 1000–1300, and 1700–1900, Closed Aug. TF. WS. E. T.

The historic bodega of Marqués de Riscal in Elciego was the birthplace of the modern Rioja wine industry.

CENICERO
Bodegas Berberana Ctra Elciego, Cenicero. Tel: 45 41 00 (Rafael Alvero). Mon-Fri 0800–1300, 1400–1700. Closed Aug. TF. WS. E. T. High-technology winery.
Bodegas Riojanas 26350 Cenicero. Tel: (Madrid) 270 56 00 (Jaime Artacho). Mon-Fri 0800–1300, 1500–1800. Closed first week Sep. TF. WS. T.
Unión-Viti-Vinícola, Bodegas Marqués de Cceres Ctra de Logroño, Cenicero. Tel: 45 40 00 (Sñra Anne Valejo). Mon-Fri 0900–1330, 1500–1800. Closed first three weeks Aug. TF. WS. E. T. Ageing barrels.

Jean Pineau and Riscal

Pineau was originally employed by the authorities of Alava to advise the province's grape farmers and small wine-makers. The measures he suggested were expensive, particularly the ageing of wine in oak barrels and the replanting of vineyards with French grape varieties, and were beyond the means of the region's small producers. It was just as his bags were packed to go home that Pineau was approached by Camilo Hurtado de Amézaga, the Marqués de Riscal, and commissioned to design a winery, using those of Bordeaux as a model. Many of his innovations are now outdated, but the winery that he built still stands as a testimony to the French contribution.

Elciego's other bodega

Just up the road is another interesting firm, Bodegas Murua Entrena. This company was formed by one man who joined up several of the town's smaller companies and he now processes some 60 per cent of the parish's harvest. As the original buildings have been sensitively restored, a visit is worthwhile.

Cenicero

From Elciego it is a 15-minute drive along a bumpy but scenic road to Cenicero on the N232, and back into the Rioja Alta. Near the railway station is another of the giants of the Riojan industry, Bodegas Berberana. The firm was originally founded in Ollauri up the road where it still has some old cellars. But its winery in Cenicero, open to visitors who have made an appointment in advance, is also well worth visiting, as it is one of the most modern in the region, with high-technology crushing and vinification equipment.

Bodegas Riojanas

A few minutes away a complete contrast is found. Firstly the tiny 'boutique' winery of Bodegas Vélazquez, and secondly, on the town's main road, is Bodegas Riojanas, originally built in 1890 by French technicians. What is appealing about this establishment is its combination of the old and the new. Stainless steel tanks rise alongside old oak vats, and the modern bottling line lies beside rows of old oak barrels. The firm produces a comprehensive range of excellent wines that are representative of the region as a whole.

Bodegas Marqués de Cáceres

Just around the corner on the eastern approach to the town is the last but

in many ways the most important of Cenicero's bodegas, Marqués de Cáceres. Here we find more recent French influence as the firm is partly owned and run by the charming Franco-Spanish Forner family who also own the prestigious Château Camensac in Bordeaux.

When the company was founded in the early 1970s, it soon became one of the region's great innovators, introducing methods of ageing and production that were in current use in Bordeaux, such as a short period of oak ageing for the reds and the fermentation and release of whites and rosés with no ageing at all. Regarded as revolutionary at the time, these methods have now been imitated by many companies.

A cellarman of Bodegas Riojanas (one of the oldest wineries in Cenicero) monitors the wine's development.

Ollauri and Haro

From Cenicero, the N232 continues its steady rise to the town of Haro. Some 2km (over a mile) from the first exit, there is a turn-off to the South that leads to the quiet hamlet of Ollauri. If you can arrange a visit to the Paternina winery, this could be one of the highlights of a tour of the Rioja.

Ollauri and Paternina

Federico Paternina is the last of the four large companies of the region, with a modern complex on the outskirts of Haro. But its deep, underground cellars at Ollauri, dug by Portuguese workers during the 16th century, are one of the Rioja's great showpieces. There is something almost frightening about them, with their long, low corridors, their blackened, musty, dripping walls and their bins of old bottles.

Haro and its bodegas

Travelling on up the road, you come to the buzzing, prosperous town of Haro. This is the centre of the Rioja Alta, and the capital of the Denomination, with one of the leading oenological stations in Spain, and numerous wine companies and fine restaurants.

If you are approaching from the East, you may be tempted to take the first signposted exit, entering the town through some ugly suburbs and ending up somewhere in the maze of streets around the central square. But it is much better to continue on the N232, passing a hotel, to the second exit which leaves the road in a broad arc to the right and then crosses over a bridge. This will lead you straight to the quarter around the railway station, the area with the greatest concentration of

HARO
Bodegas Muga Barrio de la Estación, Haro. Tel: 31 04 98 (Sñra Maria-Angeles Garcia). Mon-Fri 1000, 1200, 1600 (in summer, 1000 and 1200). Closed Jun 24–30 and Sep 8–13. Oak barrels, vats. TF. WS. T.

Compañia Vinícola del Norte de España Av Costa del Vino 21, 26200 Haro. Tel: 31 06 50 (*Encargado visitas* – visits organizer). Mon-Fri 1000–1300, 1600–1800. Closed Aug. TF. WS. T. Old machinery.
La Rioja Alta Barrio de la Estación, Haro. Tel: 31 28 54 (Sñrta Gabriela Rezola). Mon-Fri 1000–1300, 1500–1700. Closed Aug. WS. E. T. Cooperage, oak barrels.

Recommended wine shop:
González Muga Pl. de la Pax 5, Haro.

Recommended restaurant:
Mesón Terete Lucrecia Arama 17, Haro. Tel: 22 31 00 33. Traditional Riojan food.

Recommended hotel:
Parador Nacional de Santo Domingo de la Calzada. Tel: 34 03 00.

Federico Paternina take great pride in their cellars carved out of the rock beneath the hamlet of Ollauri in the 16th century. They are a national monument in the Rioja.

bodegas. Many of them are very prestigious companies with old traditions and varied histories.

First, there is the tastefully modernized but traditional and highly respected La Rioja Alta which has recently been expanded. Across the road is López de Heredia with its fairytale Swiss tower, a firm that prides itself on its unbroken adherence to traditional methods of production and ageing, and whose winery is virtually a working museum. There is the larger, very prestigious Compañía Vinícola del Norte de España (C.V.N.E.), which produces a wide range of high quality wines embracing all the different styles produced in the region. Bodegas Bilbainas has the most extensive underground cellars in the Rioja, while the charming, almost magical Bodegas Muga has a winery housed in lovely old sandstone buildings, almost a monument to the oak barrel and the vat.

All of these companies, regarded by many as the real aristocrats of the Rioja, are well worth visiting. The other, more modern wineries south of the town tend to pale into insignificance.

The town centre
Haro is also a town worth wandering around, and it is a good place to stay overnight. It has a pleasant central square surrounded by arcades, with old houses dating back to the 18th century. The church of Santo Tomás is older. Accommodation can be found either at the unpretentious Hostal Iturrimuri on the N232 or at the great Parador at Santo Domingo de la Calzada some 15 minutes' drive out of town.

Furthermore, the town has some good, traditional restaurants, including the famous Mesón Terete in the centre. Specializing in lamb roasted in a baker's oven, and served at simple wooden tables, it is a must for all travellers in the Rioja.

Further travel
To continue from the Rioja to the wine regions of Old Castile, the traveller can take the N111 from Logroño and then the N122 after Soria to Aranda de Duero. Or, and this is the suggested route, particularly in the winter, follow the N232 or the A68 northwards and join the A1 or N1 which lead down to the historic city of Burgos. From there the N1 goes straight to Aranda.

One of Haro's most famous landmarks is the tower of the López de Heredia winery in the Barrio de la Estación area.

Food and Festivals

An elaborately framed menu outside Mesón Terete in Haro announces regional dishes such as tender roast lamb (see page 39).

RIOJAN CUISINE

The excellence of Riojan cuisine is based on the sheer quality of its raw materials. Fresh fish is brought down from the Basque coast, lamb is reared in the hills of the Alta and Alavesa. The Baja is one of the great gardens of Spain, producing excellent vegetables: artichokes, asparagus, tomatoes, lettuce and peppers.

Lamb occupies a central position in the local cuisine. Dishes range from the classic *Cordero asado* to lamb chops grilled over a fire of vine shoots, another regional favourite. The local *chorizo*, not as spicy as in the rest of Spain, adds bite to stews such as *Patatas a la Riojana*.

The arrival of the year's first asparagus is an important date in the region's gastronomic calendar. Peppers, preferably the famous *pimientos del pico*, make an appearance in most local meals, either in stews, or baked or fried and served alongside meat, or stuffed with various other ingredients. The

FOOD SPECIALITIES

Callos a la Riojana Tripe cooked with whole *chorizos*, ham, nuts and several different vegetables and spices.
Chuleta de Ternera a la Riojana This dish is typical of the region as it combines grilled meat, in this case veal chops, sprinkled with chopped garlic and parsley, and peppers.
Menestra de Verduras A great local favourite which combines the region's wonderful vegetables – artichokes, peas and asparagus – together with cured ham and eggs which are either hard boiled or beaten into the mixture.

Cordero asado Lamb baked in an earthenware dish and served with a salad – try the baby lettuce split in half and mixed with vinaigrette, garlic and anchovies.
Patatas a la Riojana A simple and hearty potato stew cooked with *chorizo*, garlic, onion and sometimes a little white wine.
Pimientos rellenos de Codornices Peppers stuffed with quails.
Solomillo al vino de Rioja One of the only great local dishes with wine used in its preparation. Beef steaks are macerated in red wine and brandy and are cooked with mushrooms and small onions.

greatest vegetable dish, however, is the *Menestra de Verduras* which shows off the local produce at its very best.

WINE FESTIVALS

Virtually every town in the Rioja has a patron saint's day which is a public holiday when the bars and streets are full until the early hours of the morning and the *zurracapote* flows. This is a mixture of wine, fruit and cinnamon which is prepared by the small wine-makers of the town and is offered to friends and visitors to drink on the premises.

The two main festivals, however, take place in Haro and Logroño.

The first is the famous 'Batalla del Vino' on St Peter's Day, 29 June. It starts with a ceremony at the chapel of San Felices, some 3km (2 miles) from Haro. Then the participants, usually dressed in white, return on foot to Haro, literally drenching each other with wine.

By comparison, the 'Feria de San Mateo' in Logroño on St Matthew's Day, 21 September, is a rather subdued affair. Traditionally it was supposed to mark the beginning of the *vendimia* but, these days, it is usually well under way by then. This is a serious religious festival, but afterwards there is plenty of jollity – and drinking – in the streets.

The Batalla del Vino *attracts hordes of local people. The participants make their way back to Haro from San Felices, squirting each other with wine from wineskins as they go.*

Aragon _____

teeped in history, the ancient Kingdom of Aragon lies between Catalonia to the East and the great vineyards of the Rioja Baja and Navarra to the West. It is believed that its wine industry dates back to the 3rd century BC when its people drank wine mixed with honey and, today, it has some 33,000 hectares of vineyard, most of which are planted to the West and South of Zaragoza, the capital.

The region produces mostly red wines, which are usually almost purple in colour with immense body and alcohol, and are high in tannins. In a tradition that goes back to the time of the phylloxera in France, many of these are used for blending. And, as the province is dominated by its co-operatives, it is neither the most dynamic nor advanced of Spain's wine regions. Each of its three Denominations, however, hides its odd gem, and these, combined with the majesty of its flat, ochre-coloured plains to the South and its views over the foothills of the Pyrenees to the North, offer a fair reward to the wine traveller en route from the Rioja or Navarra to Catalonia.

Aragon's harsh climate and rocky landscape tend to preserve the older way of life. Many of the villages of central Aragon have changed little in the past century.

The route outlined below is for drivers entering the region from Navarra or the Rioja Baja, and leads in a zig-zag from west to east. Those entering from Catalonia can follow the route in reverse.

From Cintruénigo where the tour of Navarra ended, drivers are advised to rejoin either the N232 or the A68, follow it to Magallón (about 50km or 30 miles) and continue to Borja.

From Borja, the centre of the Campo de Borja Denomination, the small C220 leads to Cariñena (60km or 37 miles), capital of the largest Denomination.

Then it is up the N330 to Zaragoza where travellers can either enter the city or use the well-signposted ring road system to the N123 that leads to Huesca (120km or 70 miles altogether). Here one enters the city before branching off on to the N240 to the Denomination of Somontano.

42

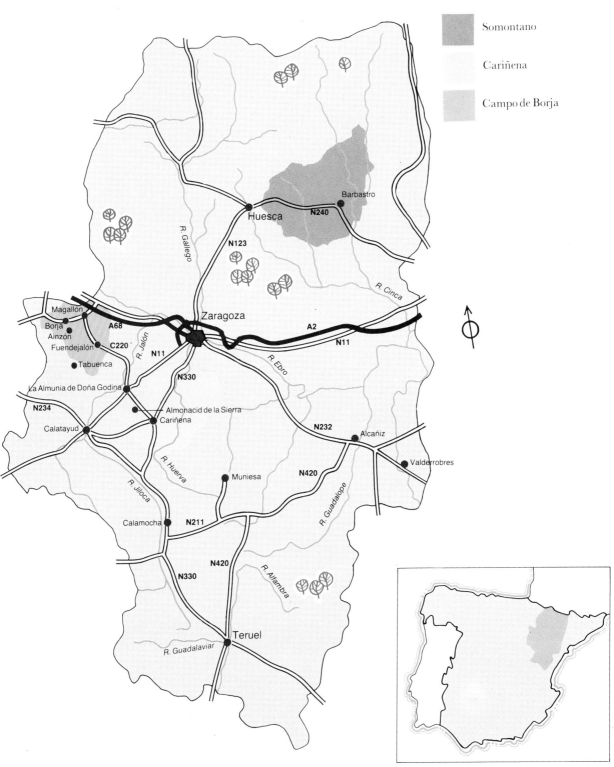

Somontano

Cariñena

Campo de Borja

Barbastro

N240

Huesca

N123

R. Gállego

R. Cinca

Magallón

A68

Zaragoza

A2

Borja

Ainzón

C220

R. Jalón

N11

N11

Fuendejalón

R. Ebro

Tabuenca

La Almunia de Doña Godina

N330

N234

Almonacid de la Sierra

Calatayud

Cariñena

N232

Alcañiz

R. Huerva

Valderrobres

Muniesa

N420

R. Guadalope

R. Jiloca

Calamocha

N211

N420

R. Alfambra

N330

Teruel

R. Guadalaviar

Wines and Wine Villages of Aragon

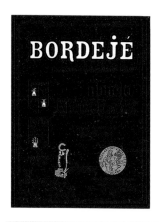

AINZON
Bodegas Bordejé S.A.T.
Ctra Borja/Rueda Km 3,
Ainzón. Tel: 86 80 80
(Fernando Bordejé). Daily
0900–1900. TF. WS. T.
Murals, cellars.

ALMONACID
**Bodegas Cavas López
Pelayo** Cerro Bodegas s/n,
Almonacid de la Sierra.
Tel: 62 70 15 (Sñr López
Pelayo). Mon-Sat
1500–2000. Closed July
25–Aug 15. TF. WS. E. Old
underground cellars.

BARBASTRO
Bodegas Fábregas Clle
Graus 14/Cerler 3,
Barbastro. Tel: 31 04 98
(Pedro Fábregas). Mon-Fri
0900–1330, 1620–1930, Sat
0930–1330. TF. WS. T.

CARINENA
Heredad Balbino Lacosta
Hermana Matilde 31–33,
Cariñena. Tel: 62 03 89
(Alberto Lacosta). Daily
0800–1500. Closed Aug.
TF. WS. T. E.

RADIQUERO
Bodegas Monclus
Radiquero. Tel: 31 81 20
(Sñrta Mercedes Monclus).
Mon-Fri 0900–1300,
1700–1900. TF. WS. T.

The 10,000 hectares of Campo de Borja, the most westerly of Aragon's D.O.s, surround the wine towns of Fuendejalón, Magallón, Borja, Ainzón and Tabuenca. Each has its big co-operative with the largest and most advanced at Borja on the Zaragoza-Soria road. These co-operatives dominate the Denomination's production, making sound reds and rosés which can be pleasant and fruity drinking when they are young. But they are dark, lugubrious places to visit.

More interesting is Bodegas Bordejé in Ainzón. This is a privately-owned firm housed in old buildings on the outskirts of the town with deep, underground cellars built towards the end of the 18th century. And it makes what is generally regarded as the best CAVA of the region as well as some interesting, oak-aged *reservas*.

Cariñena and Almonacid
From Ainzón, take the C220, which leads directly to the town of Cariñena, the centre of the Denomination of the same name. With its inexpensive hotel and a good restaurant on its outskirts serving regional food, this is a convenient town in which to stay overnight.

It also has two bodegas that are worth a visit. The first is the great co-operative of San Valero on the N330 to Teruel which produces a good range of wines in its massive installations in different parts of the town. And the second is the smaller, family-owned Heredad Balbino Lacosta. This is an estate winery, producing some of the best wines of the region from grapes grown on its own vineyards in a charming, compact winery built in the 1940s.

Another good place to visit is Bodegas López Pelayo, the oldest bodega in the region, which is hidden away in Almonacid de la Sierra some 10km (6 miles) away. This is a tiny winery but its cobweb-encrusted cellars were dug in the rock with pick-axes over 300 years ago and have hardly been altered since.

The wines
As Cariñena and Campo de Borja share the same climate and soil structures, and are dependent on the same grape, their wines are broadly similar. Curiously the Cariñena, which is still used in Catalonia, is no longer important in this part of Aragon. The extremes of climate, with baking hot summers and numbing cold winters, have ensured that the hardy Garnacha reigns supreme producing robust, hard and

strong wines that soften with age. Further north in the province of Huesca, however, the tiny Denomination of Somontano produces wines that have a very different character. Lying in the foothills of the Pyrenees, it is higher and its soils are lighter. Most importantly, however, it has a greater variety of grapes, with noble French varieties such as the Cabernet Sauvignon, the Merlot and the Chardonnay mingling with the excellent local Moristrel. Somontano may be a small Denomination with only four firms, but it produces some excellent wines.

The bodegas of Somontano
The largest of these firms is the Co-operativa de Somontano de Sobrabe on the road to Naval just outside Barbastro. By Spanish standards it is a small co-operative, but it accounts for 90 per cent of the region's production. And, although its winery is not very interesting, it produces top quality wines.

Just a few kilometres down the same road is Bodegas Lalanne. Built in 1847 by a French family, this is a leafy, ramshackle place, more like a Latin American *hacienda* than a winery. But it produces an excellent range of wines, many of them made with French varieties.

Finally, there are two very much smaller, family-owned firms, Bodegas Fábregas in Barbastro and Bodegas Monclus in Radiquero, just up the road from Lalanne. Again, both produce excellent wines.

From Barbastro the N240 leads to Lérida and the turn-off to Raimat (see page 111) is about 10km (6 miles) from the city.

Almonacid de la Sierra is the home of Bodegas López Pelayo.

RECOMMENDED RESTAURANTS:

BARBASTRO
Restaurante Flor Clle Goya 3, Barbastro. Tel: 31 10 56. '*Haute cuisine*'. Expensive.

CARINENA
Mesón El Escudo on the C220 on the outskirts of Cariñena. No booking needed. Typically Aragonese cuisine.

HUESCA
Venta El Soton Ctra Tarragona-San Sebastian Km 226, Esquedas, Huesca. Tel: 27 02 41. Situated in a small village outside Huesca. Typically Aragonese cuisine.

Old Castile and Galicia

Known in modern times as Castilla-León, Old Castile was the heartland of Spain in the Middle Ages. It was here that the Christian rulers of northern Spain finally forged a united Spain (through the marriage of Isabella, Queen of Castile, to King Ferdinand of Aragon, in 1469), paving the way to the defeat of the last Moorish bastion in the peninsula, the city of Granada; and it was here that the united Spaniards established their political and religious centre, a foundation for one of the world's greatest empires. This is a region that offers a great deal to the tourist – mighty castles, mediaeval cities and innumerable churches and monasteries. Its simple cuisine is justly famous, and it is an important wine-producing region.

It must be remembered, however, that Old Castile lies on the *meseta*, the highest plateau in Europe. Most of it is over 600 metres (2,000ft) above sea level, and the climate is extreme, with temperatures rising to 40°C in the summer and plunging to –20°C in the winter. It is best, therefore, to make this trip in spring or autumn, when conditions will be at their best.

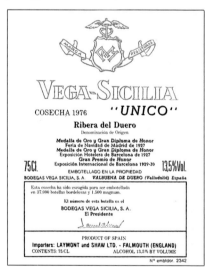

The route to Old Castile

From Haro where the tour of the Rioja ended, there is a journey north of 10km (6 miles) before you reach the beginning of the A1 *autopista*, which heads down to Burgos, the first great city of Old Castile. The toll-free N1 runs almost parallel.

The Ribera del Duero

From Burgos the N1 leads straight to Aranda de Duero, 75km (47 miles) away, which is the starting point of the route through the Ribera del Duero. This is straightforward – you simply follow the N122 to Valladolid, with optional detours to the small towns of Pedrosa and Pesquera along the way.

Toro and Rueda

Tordesillas, 25km (16 miles) south of Valladolid, is a convenient base for trips to Toro and Rueda, the capitals of their Denominations. Thereafter, the road heads for Madrid.

For those with little time to spare, the NVI leads south to the town of Adanero, where it is possible to join the A6. Both roads then cross the Sierra de Guadarrama to Madrid. During the winter, and particularly in snow, the *autopista* is recommended.

Segovia

For those with more time, one or two days spent exploring the mountain villages of Segovia can be very rewarding. From Medina del Campo, the small C112 leads eastwards to the towns of Sepúlveda, Riaza and Pedraza. The N110 then leads back to Segovia. From there, the A603 joins the A6 or the NVI which takes you across the Sierra.

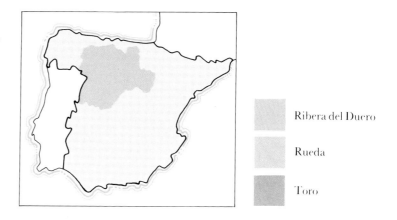

	Ribera del Duero
	Rueda
	Toro

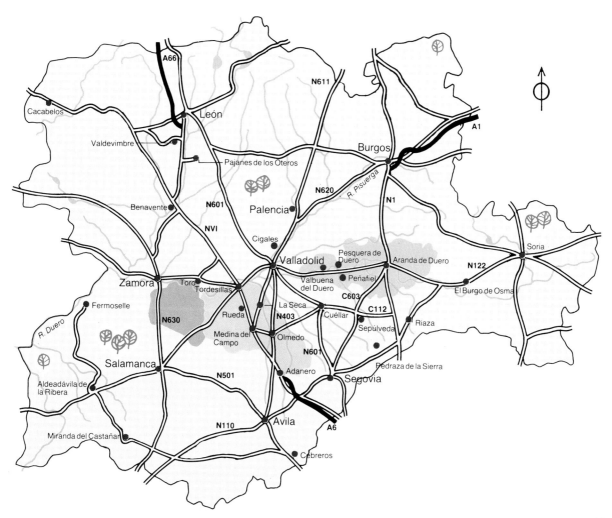

The Wines of Old Castile

A woman wheels her barrow through the old village of Peñafiel.

Ribera del Duero

Granted its status as a Denomination in 1983, the Ribera del Duero's wine-growing area is expanding and has now reached about 12,000 hectares. The vineyards follow the river valley, but most are concentrated in the area of Aranda de Duero. The Tinto Fino (also known as the Tinto del País, a variant of the Tempranillo) holds pride of place in the region, though it is sometimes blended with other authorized varieties such as the Garnacha and the Albillo.

Toro

Toro has only been delimited since 1987 and embraces vineyards in the provinces of Valladolid and Zamora. The principal grape variety is the red Tinta de Toro which covers some 40 per cent of the vineyard area. The red Tinto Madrid (also known as the Negral) is also authorized, as is the Malvasía used in the production of the region's white wines.

The wine industry of Old Castile dates back to the Visigothic period. By the 13th century its wines were quenching the thirst of the countless pilgrims who made their way to Santiago de Compostela. And, when the Catholic monarchs transferred the court to Valladolid, it reached a peak of prosperity. The ancient town of Medina del Campo boasted some 470 wine merchants. Columbus is said to have taken casks of Toro on his first great voyage of discovery. When the court moved to Madrid, the region lost its pre-eminence, but its wine industry continued to prosper, selling to the vineless provinces of northern Spain.

The vineyards' retreat

During the past century the region has suffered two major disasters. First, at the turn of the century, came phylloxera, devastating the region's vineyards. Then, in the late 1930s, at the end of the Civil War, new Wheat Laws were passed to encourage more wheat production. As a result, Old Castile became Spain's 'bread basket' at the expense of the vineyards.

The variety of wines

The region still produces an immense amount of wine, and in many different styles: there are, for example, the light and subtle wines of El Bierzo; the famous *claretes* of Cigales, to the North of Valladolid; and the strongly *pétillant* 'needle wines' or *vinos de aguja* of León. More importantly, the region has three Denominations of Origin: Rueda, Toro, and the Ribera del Duero. These are small regions and have lain in comparative obscurity for some years. But investment has begun to flow and their potential is generally regarded as enormous.

The Ribera

The largest of these Denominations is the Ribera del Duero which lies on the river Duero to the East of Valladolid. Until recently it was best known abroad for Vega Sicilia, perhaps the most celebrated and certainly the most expensive of Spanish red wines. Highly perfumed and with a wonderful balance between concentrated and fragrant fruit, and an oakiness acquired after long periods of barrel ageing, these wines have always enjoyed immense prestige in Spain. Other less famous firms, often producing rather different wines, are slowly coming to the fore in this area. And there are those who believe that eventually the region may produce the best red wines in Spain.

Many of the wines are made exclusively from the Tinto Fino grape (see Ribera data panel, left),

but this is sometimes blended with the other Spanish varieties, the Garnacha and the Albillo (a white variety often used in the production of *claretes*). The influence of Vega Sicilia has also resulted in the authorization of Merlot, Cabernet Sauvignon and Malbec. But plantings of these are small and even at Vega they only account for about 35 percent of the total *coupage*, or blend of grape varieties.

Toro and Rueda

Toro lies further to the West in the province of Zamora and its wines are very different: thick with tannin and extract, bursting with fruit and with a high level of alcohol. A very special, perhaps an acquired taste!

Finally, there is Rueda, a region famous for its fortified wines. Aged in carboy (a huge rounded glass bottle), or transferred from barrel to barrel to produce wines of a uniform character and quality, they recall the wines of Jerez and Montilla. Since the opening of Marqués de Riscal's winery in 1972, however, production of light white table wines has increased. Crisp, delicate, and fruity, they are made for modern tastes.

The story of Old Castile is still one of potential more than anything else. It does already produce some outstanding wines, but the quantity is still small. If investment continues, however, there can be little doubt that a powerful new force will soon emerge in the Spanish wine industry.

The church of San Pablo in Peñafiel dates back to Romanesque times.

Rueda

The Denomination of Rueda covers about 4,000 hectares in the provinces of Segovia, Valladolid and Avila. Although there are still substantial plantings of Palomino, the Verdejo has now taken over as the region's top grape variety with over 50 per cent of the vineyard area.

There are two types of table wines, Rueda, and Rueda Superior, and two *generosos*, Pálido and Dorado Ruedo.

The Ribera del Duero

The Ribera del Duero stretches along the banks of the mighty river Duero from El Burgo de Osma to Tudela del Duero. The Ribera is the highest of Old Castile's Denominations, and just nudges the altitude limit for grape-growing. Its vines are planted on the protected slopes of the fertile river valley.

The river valley, with its mists and pine trees, has a special microclimate and is one of the reasons for the exceptional quality of the wines. The other is the grapes, for although the Cabernet Sauvignon, the Malbec and the Merlot are authorized, and are planted at Vega Sicilia, it is the Tinto Fino which is the most widely used. With a little Albillo, this produces wines with fine balance, delicate fruit and an intense aroma. Oak-ageing makes them smoother and more rounded too.

Aranda de Duero

Coming from the Rioja, the first stop is Aranda de Duero. This quiet, typically Castilian town has good hotels. The Mesón de la Villa, one of the best restaurants in the area, serves excellent regional dishes.

The first important wine firm of the Ribera, the Torremilanos estate, is on the edge of the town, set in its own vineyards. It produces excellent wines, lighter than usual, with the emphasis on bottle rather than barrel-ageing. The bodega dates back to the turn of the century.

If you have time, a detour to the small town of Pedrosa is worthwhile. This is the home of the modern firm of Hermanos Pérez Pascuas.

Otherwise, continue on down the N122 to Peñafiel, passing Vega Sicilia on the way. Unfortunately,

although it is Spain's most prestigious winery, it is closed to the public and does not sell wine on the premises.

Peñafiel and Pesquera

The small town of Peñafiel lies at the junction of three valleys, and its mighty 14th-century castle is a landmark. The Asador Mauro is an excellent place for lunch. This is also

the home of the region's best co-operative, on the main road at the entrance to the town. It produces excellent, traditional wines, some aged for up to 10 years in oak.

The last visit to make on this tour of the Ribera is to Bodegas Alejandro Fernández, in the hamlet of Pesquera de Duero, on the road from Peñafiel to Palencia. Although it is not much to look at, this is a

firm that has recently been hitting the headlines: while the traditional houses age their wines for long periods in oak, this firm ages its wines for two years maximum in barrel and for a long time in bottle. Oak flavours are more subtle and the wines gain in complexity.

After Pesquera, return to the N122 which takes you onward to the historic city of Valladolid.

Deep under Peñafiel's mediaeval castle the local wine co-operative has excavated cellars from the rock to house their traditional wines.

Valladolid, Tordesillas and Toro

*Toro's wines 'with character' (*personalidad*) vary partly with the region's soils which range from eastern sandiness to western clay.*

Valladolid and Tordesillas

As the former capital of Castile and León, in the late Middle Ages, Valladolid has some splendid historic sites. There is the College of San Gregorio, and the great 16th-century cathedral, and the house of the great Cervantes, author of Spain's classic *Don Quijote* (*Quixote*). For devotees of food and wine there is the Mesón La Fragua, regarded as the best restaurant of the region. But Valladolid is not a good place for the driver: it is a mediaeval city, a maze of narrow streets, and its one-way systems make driving around and trying to park a nightmare.

An alternative is to stay at Tordesillas which is 35km (22 miles) away on the N620. This is another historic little town built on a hill – it was here that Spain and Portugal divided the New World between them in 1494. The Convent of Santa Clara, where Joanna the Mad (died 1555), imprisoned by her son the Emperor Charles V, spent the last 40 years of her life, is well worth a visit. There is also a very fine Parador Nacional on the N122, on the outskirts of the town.

The town of Toro

From Tordesillas the town of Toro is 40km (25 miles) along the N122. It is an interesting town with old buildings and an arcaded central square lined with shops and small bars. To the North the great wheat fields of Spain begin to roll, a land known as the 'Tierra del Pan'. To the South are the vineyards in the 'Tierra del Vino'.

A small Denomination, Toro has only a handful of firms, the most important being Bodegas Fariña. Its old cellars are in the small town of Casaseca de las Chanas. In the town

of Toro itself, Fariña is in the process of building a brand new, purpose-built winery for its bottling and vinification.

Modern developments in Toro

Toro has always been famous in Spain for its big red wines (see page 49). Traditionally, these are almost black in colour, packed with tannin and extract, fruity and very alcoholic.

However, things are changing. The grape-growers are now encouraged to pick earlier to reduce the alcohol levels in the wine, and the period in which the skins are left in contact with the must is being reduced, to make the wines a little lighter. Stainless steel is now installed for cold fermentation and the classic 225-litre oak barrel is beginning to replace the massive cherry and chestnut barrels of the past. The red wines are certainly improving and are becoming more accessible and elegant, while maintaining their great character. The whites, made from the Malvasía, are also worth trying.

Rueda

Rueda, Old Castile's great white wine-producing Denomination, lies

The facade of San Pablo is one of a number of striking architectural masterpieces in Valladolid, including the cathedral and one of Spain's oldest universities.

to the South of Valladolid. The capital of the Denomination, the town of Rueda itself, is an easy 10km (6 mile) drive from Tordesillas. It is a dusty, unexciting place, but the line of wine shops along the main street underline its commitment to wine production.

Rueda

RUEDA
**Bodegas de Crianza
Castilla la Vieja S.A.** Ctra
Madrid-La Coruña Km
170. Tel: 86 81 16/86 83 36
(Antonio Sanz). Mon-Fri
0700–1500 (summer);
0900– 1300, and 1500–1900
(rest of the year). TF. WS.
T.
**Vinos Blancos de Castilla
S.A.** Ctra NVI Km 172,
Rueda. Tel: 86 80 29
(Francisco Hurtado). Mon-
Fri 0900–1300, 1500– 1900.
Closed Aug. TF. WS. E. T.
High-technology winery.

*Each of the D.O. Rueda's wines displays the
8-spoked cartwheel symbol. Rueda (above) is
made from 25 per cent Verdejo grapes, and
varies in alcohol from 11.5 to 14 per cent.*

*The Pálido is the strongest of Rueda's
celebrated generosos or fortified wines, with
15 per cent alcohol. The style recalls the
generosos of Montilla and Jerez.*

Rueda's *generosos*

Rueda is fortunate to have survived
the phylloxera. In the province of
Valladolid alone some 55,000
hectares of vineyard were lost, and
many were never replanted. And the
phylloxera had a long-lasting effect:
because of its higher productivity, the
Palomino grape became the most
widely planted variety, and the whole
emphasis of production was
switched from table wines to fortified
or *generoso* wines, aged in barrel or
glass carboy (huge rounded bottle),
and bearing a vague similarity to the
wines of Jerez and Montilla.

These *generosos* come in two styles:
the Dorado Rueda has an alcoholic
strength of 14 per cent, and is aged
for a minimum of four years, two of
which must be in oak barrel. The
Pálido Rueda has an alcoholic
strength of 15 per cent and is aged
also for a minimum of four years,
but three of these must be in oak.

Both styles can be identified by their
back label, and are popular
throughout the North of the country.

Rueda's table wines

Recently, however, Rueda has begun
to change direction. In the early
1970s the great Riojan house of
Marqués de Riscal announced that
it was transferring its white wine
production to this region.

The reason for partly abandoning
the Rioja was simple: it was felt that
the Verdejo, which is native to Old
Castile, had greater potential than
the Viura and was capable of
producing white wines of sufficient
quality to put alongside its great
Riojan reds and rosés.

Riscal's purpose-built, space-age
style winery on the northern
outskirts of the town is impressive.
The Verdejo is a delicate variety,
and the latest grape crushers were
installed, working very gently on the

Like the Pálido, the Dorado generoso *relies on the* crianza, *the oak barrel, and on the region's traditional grapes, Verdejo and Palomino, for its colour.*

Rueda Superior is made with a minimum of 60 per cent Verdejo or Sauvignon Blanc (though most have more than that). Like Rueda, it varies from 11.5 to 14 per cent alcohol.

Queen Isabella, one of Spain's most famous monarchs, was a frequent visitor here at the mighty castle of La Mota in Medina del Campo (page 56).

grapes. Stainless steel tanks were also introduced, for cold fermentation, which preserves fruit and aroma.

The results are a revelation: wines of great fragrance, with lovely delicate fruit and a refreshing edge of acidity. Nor has Riscal stopped here. Recently it has released a Sauvignon Blanc from grapes grown in its own vineyards, well worth trying.

Other bodegas

Encouraged by Riscal's success, other local firms have begun investing and have looked again at their table wines. The most important of these is Bodegas de Crianza Castilla la Vieja at the southern limit of the town. Its winery is ramshackle, but it produces a wide range of *generosos* and table wines, the best of which are 'New Wave' whites bottled under the Marqués de Griñon label. The huge co-operative in nearby La Seca is also of interest.

The Mountains of Segovia

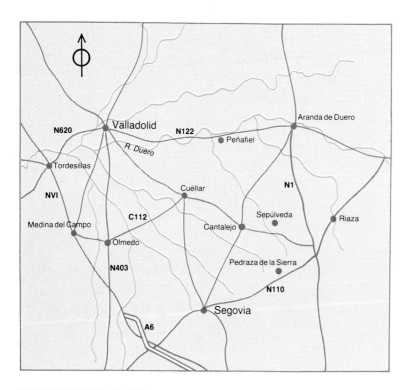

Spain, died in 1504. Then take the small C112 that leads east from Medina towards Sepúlveda.

The *hornos de asar*

Old Castile has always been famous for its roasting ovens or *hornos de asar*. These are made with bricks or mud in a conical shape, and are used to bake bread or roast meat. They are heated with fires of pine wood, vine shoots or eucalyptus. The results are magnificent: large, round, golden loaves and succulent, tender lamb and suckling pig.

Sepúlveda and Riaza

Sepúlveda is 110km (68 miles) from Medina del Campo through lush hills and pine forests. It is a picturesque old town, perfumed with the scent of wood fires and roast meat, a popular lunching spot with numerous inexpensive and unpretentious restaurants. The most famous of these is Casa Tinín near the centre: this restaurant is famous for its lamb, killed before it is a month old and roasted in large glazed earthenware dishes.

An alternative to Sepúlveda is Riaza on the other side of the N1. Recently, wealthy Madrileños have crowded its outskirts with their weekend homes, but its centre remains reasonably unspoilt, with an interesting circular plaza ringed by an arcade of quaint bars and cafés. It doubles as a bullring during the town's annual fiesta. Its restaurants can be equally recommended.

Segovia

Regaining the N1 after Riaza, follow it for a short distance, and then turn west on to the N110 to Segovia. On the way, a detour to the charming

MEDINA DEL CAMPO
Recommended restaurant:
Restaurante Madrid
Claudio Moyano 2, Medina del Campo. Tel: 80 01 34. Typically Castilian.

SEGOVIA
Recommended restaurants:
Duque Maestro Asador
Clle Cervantes 12, Segovia. Tel: 43 05 37. Roasts.
Mesón de Cándido Plaza del Azoguejo 5, Segovia. Tel: 42 59 11. Roast suckling pig.

SEPULVEDA
Recommended restaurant:
Casa Tinín Sepúlveda. Ask any passerby for directions. Roast lamb is the speciality.

From Valladolid or Tordesillas the route heads directly south to Madrid. There are no wine towns or wineries on this leg of the journey, but the area is renowned in Spain for its gastronomy, and a little extra driving can lead to some truly memorable meals. This is also an area of great beauty, with lovely old towns, some of which have almost been abandoned, while others seem to continue in their old ways, hardly touched by passing centuries.

Medina del Campo

For those interested in history, it is worth making a short stop at Medina del Campo just to the South of Tordesillas. This was an important wine town in the Middle Ages, and here you can visit the castle of La Mota where the great Queen Isabella, who married Ferdinand of Aragon and thus united

old town of Pedraza de la Sierra with its old houses and cobbled streets, is an absolute must.

Segovia itself is a magnificent city, and it is worth spending some time there to visit its sights, which include one of the finest Roman aqueducts in Europe, the fascinating Alcázar and a charming Old Town or *Ciudad Vieja*. It is also the home of Old Castile's other great dish, roast suckling pig or *Cochinillo asado*. Again, one of the great secrets is that the animal is killed when only about three weeks old, and is then roasted

slowly in a large oven. In the city's most famous restaurant, the Mesón de Cándido near the aqueduct, eucalyptus is burned in the roasting oven, and the result is incomparable.

Further travel

From Segovia, return to the A6 *autopista*; this is a good road on which to cross the great Sierra de Guadarrama, but it should be avoided in mid-winter. Detours to the Escorial and the Valle de los Caidos, both hidden in the mountains, are highly recommended.

Riaza's main plaza, with its town hall in the centre, is the scene of an annual bullfight.

Food and Festivals

The Mesón La Fragua in Valladolid (see page 52) is one of the best and most typical of Old Castile's restaurants. It still has its traditional large asador or roasting oven in which to prepare regional foods.

FOOD SPECIALITIES

Sopa de Ajo A garlic soup thickened with breadcrumbs, with an egg broken into the centre.

Cachelada Leónesa A hearty stew of *chorizos* and potatoes, not unlike *Patatas a la Riojana* from the Rioja. Different types of *chorizo* are used, but the most famous is from El Bierzo in the North of León.

Judías con Pie y Oreja Different types of *chorizo* and *morcilla* simply combined with white beans and pork (pig's foot and ear), popular around Segovia.

Huevos fritos con Morcilla de Sayago Fried eggs with black pudding, a good dish from around Zamora.

Estofado de Ternera a la Zamorana A delicious veal stew cooked with carrots, peas, onions and peppers, enriched with white wine and *aguardiente*.

Menestra a la Palentina The vegetable stew, best when the vegetables are young and tender. In the most sophisticated version of the dish, slices of chicken and bacon are added to the artichokes, courgettes, peas, potatoes and broad beans, and the stew is cooked in white wine.

Perdices a la Segoviana This is the typical way of cooking small game in the region. The partridges are baked in an earthenware dish, with vegetables.

Ropa Vieja (Old Clothes) Another characteristic stew from the kitchens of Old Castile made with cooked meat (chicken, pork, beef or a mixture of meats) with beans, chickpeas and a *sofrito* of fried onions, peppers and aubergines.

Rape Castellano Angler fish in a thick sauce made with onions, pine nuts and eggs. A more sophisticated version also has clams.

FESTIVALS

Old Castile has no great wine fiestas like those of the Rioja or Jerez, but most of the towns of the region have their annual fiesta, where bulls take pride of place. Bullfights can be colourful spectacles for those who can stomach them.

Particularly famous is the 'Toro de la Vega' fiesta in Tordesillas in September, an event that dates back to the 16th century. A bull is released in the town's central square and is then chased out on to the plain (the *Vega*) where it is killed by the men of the town on horseback. Not for the squeamish!

CUISINE OF OLD CASTILE

The *meseta* of Old Castile is the highest plateau of Europe, and suffers from particularly cold winters. So it will come as no surprise that the cuisine is hearty.

Meat dishes
Meat and meat products, such as the spicy sausage *chorizo* (the best of which is said to come from León) and *morcilla* (a type of black pudding), play a central role in the region's great stews such as *Cachelada* and *Ropa Vieja* (see recommended food specialities, facing page). These may be combined both with meat and beans, and fried eggs too.

The region also produces good roasting meats – lamb, suckling pig (*Cochinillo asado*) and even kid, though this is more difficult to find.

The northern part of the region between León and Valladolid produces wonderful round loaves with golden crusts and delicious soft white insides.

The area to the North of the Duero, known as the Tierra de Campos, grows excellent vegetables, the basis of the *Menestra*. Small game, particularly partridges, quail and hare, is also abundant, and is usually cooked in its own juices in an earthenware dish with vegetables.

Fish dishes
As the region is far from the coast, salt water fish is rare. Occasionally salt cod is offered, usually prepared in the oven. *Bacalao a la Tranca*, which is cooked with vegetables and spices, is an interesting version. But restaurants more usually have river fish, particularly trout which can be excellent in León and Segovia.

Castilians prepare trout in a simpler way than that of Navarra, where this is also a well-known dish – a little pork fat is used for basting, and the fish is simply grilled. It is harder to find river crabs on a menu, but well worth the search. They are cooked with a tomato sauce and with brandy, and are quite delicious (*Cangrejos de Rio*).

Roast suckling pig is a speciality in Old Castile, along with roast lamb. The meats are displayed here with a classic range of regional vegetables.

Galicia

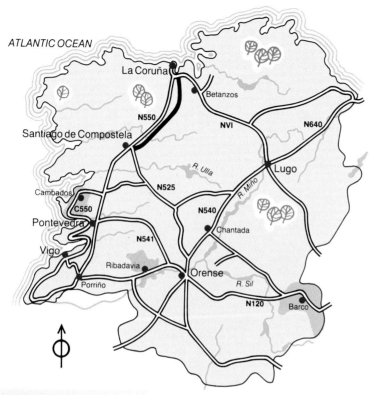

ATLANTIC OCEAN

■ Ribeiro

Valdeorras

ORENSE
Recommended restaurant:
Restaurante San Miguel
Clle San Miguel 12–14,
Orense. Tel: 22 12 45.

PONTEVEDRA
Recommended restaurant:
Casa Solla San Salvador de
Poyo s/n, Pontevedra. Tel:
85 26 78.

RIBADAVIA
**Co-operativa Vitivinícola
del Ribeiro** Valdepereira,
Ribadavia (Orense). Tel:
47 01 75 (Argimiro Levoso).
TF. WS.

**SANTIAGO DE
COMPOSTELA**
Recommended restaurant:
Restaurante Vilas Rosalia
de Castro 88, Santiago de
Compostela. Tel: 59 10 00.

Galicia is a long way from any of
Spain's other leading wine regions, at
least three hours hard driving from
León and further from Valladolid or
the Rioja. And, despite their
popularity and fame in Spain, its
wines do not merit a wide detour.
The intention here is to offer some
suggestions to travellers who are
visiting the region anyway.

Galicia's wines

Galicia's wines must be the most
confusing in Spain: they are made
from an estimated 100 different grape
varieties, and the climate is the
wettest and least predictable in the
country. Much of the wine is made
by small farmers with only
rudimentary equipment. (This *vino del
cosechero* is usually best avoided.)

At the other end of the scale,
however, the province has three
Denominations: the Ribeiro,

The cathedral of Santiago has been the destination of Christian pilgrims through the ages. The facade is a Baroque masterpiece built by Fernando Casas y Novoa in 1750, but much of the building remains mediaeval.

Garnacha. At their best the reds should be very aromatic, cherry coloured, fresh and fruity. The whites should be light in alcohol, crisp and fresh, fruity and even slightly *pétillant*. In both cases some are aged in oak, but they are usually at their best when young.

Valdeorras and the Ribeiro

Lying on the banks of the Sil River, the town of Barco is halfway between Orense and Ponferrada on the N120. This is the centre of the Denomination Valdeorraş and the home of its biggest co-operative, the Co-operativa Jesus Nazareno. The winery would not be worth visiting, were it not for its fascinating range of wines, many of them made from local varieties. These are for sale at the bodega door.

The centre of the Ribeiro is the town of Ribadavia to the West of Orense on the N120. At the end of April the town holds a small wine fair in its central park, which offers a good opportunity to taste a broad range of the region's wines. It also has a large co-operative on its outskirts which makes the best wines of the area.

Cambados

The final area of interest is around the town of Cambados on the coastal C550 route to the North of Pontevedra, which can make a pleasant detour on the route to Santiago. The town has a good Parador and is the home of several leading producers including Bodegas Chaves and Bodegas Vilariño-Cambados. So it is a good place to taste some of the Albariños wines, particularly with the excellent seafood of the area.

Valdeorras, and the Specific Denomination of Albariño for wines made within the province entirely from that variety. These wines with a guarantee of origin can be very interesting, particularly when they are made from the better regional varieties, such as the white Albariño, Treixadura, Godello and Torrontes, and the red Caino and Mencia with the less exotic Tempranillo and

New Castile

The region of Castilla La Mancha, or New Castile as it is usually known, is on the high *meseta* south of Madrid; its provinces are Toledo, Ciudad Real, Cuenca and Albacete, all of which have important wine industries.

Despite its literary connotations and the majesty of its landscape, it is a sad region, seemingly forlorn and forgotten. During the Middle Ages it was a buffer zone between the Christian North and the Muslim South. Today it plays a similar role, a no-man's-land between Madrid and Andalusia.

For the tourist interested in history or architecture, there are some splendid sites. But for the wine and food enthusiast there are fewer attractions, just the odd place of special interest hidden away in the vast, featureless plain.

This is also a difficult region to visit. Not only are the summers unbearably hot but the distances between the leading producers are often great. Valdepeñas is compact enough, as most of its wineries are in the town, but in La Mancha, the bodegas are separated by long drives, often along appalling roads.

As it leads almost directly south, the route through New Castile is comparatively straightforward. From Madrid the busy NIV leads along a dual carriageway as far as Aranjuez, where it is worth stopping for a few hours. Then the N400 leads to the fabulous city of Toledo. The small Manchegan towns of Consuegra and Puerto Lápice are only about 70km (43 miles) further south.

From a base at Alcázar de San Juan, a day trip can be taken to the towns of El Toboso, Mota del Cuervo and Villarrobledo. After this you can rejoin the NIV for Manzanares, and make a detour to Almagro. The C415 then leads south to the town of Valdepeñas, where most of the Denomination's bodegas are located.

The flat, dusty and sparsely cultivated meseta *(high plateau) of New Castile offers awesome vistas of endless space. Most of the* meseta *is covered by the D.O. La Mancha, one of the largest delimited wine zones in the world.*

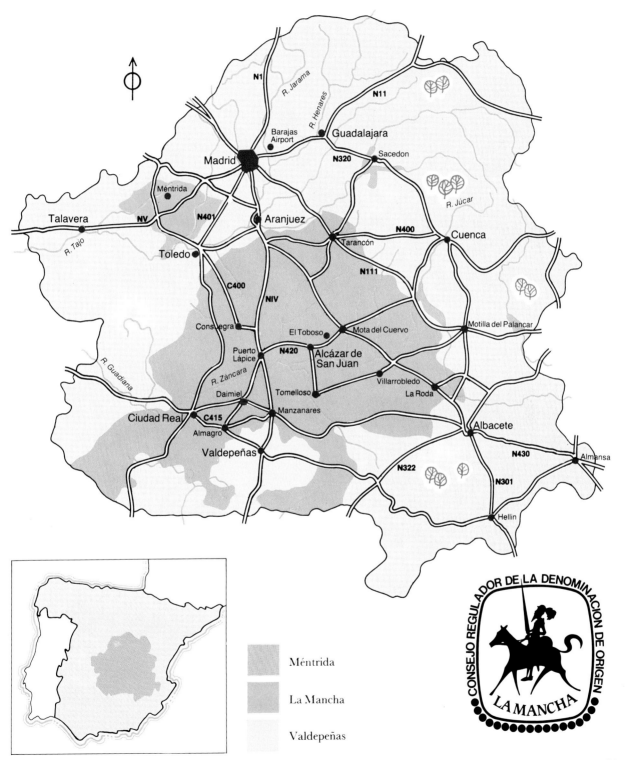

Méntrida

La Mancha

Valdepeñas

The Wines of New Castile

The Denomination of Origin of La Mancha covers some 120,000 hectares of vineyard at an altitude of about 700 metres above sea level. Around 70 per cent of production, however, takes place within a 30km (19 mile) radius of Alcázar de San Juan.

The Airén covers some 90 per cent of the vineyard area, enough to make it one of the most widely planted grape varieties of the world. Also authorized are the white Pardillo, Verdoncho and Macabeo, and the red Cencibel, Garnacha and Moravia.

The D.O. Valdepeñas covers 35,000 hectares in the southern part of the province of Ciudad Real.

The Airén still covers about 85 per cent of the vineyard area but the Cencibel, the only other authorized variety, is gaining ground.

Divided into three Denominations – Méntrida (a region in the province of Toledo, best known for its thick blending wines), Valdepeñas and La Mancha – New Castile produces an immense amount of wine. In normal years it accounts for about 40 per cent of Spain's total production, a percentage that can rise to 50 per cent when the harvests of the North are small. In area, La Mancha is the largest delimited wine region in the world, producing some 3 million hectolitres of bottled wine a year. It also produces a very much greater quantity of wine that is sold in bulk.

New Castile produces this vast quantity very cheaply indeed. As there is no shortage of space, the vines are planted well apart so the yield per hectare is low (perhaps 25 to 28 hectolitres per hectare). But vine diseases are all but banished by the dryness of the climate and the extremes of temperature. In mediaeval times this area was known as *tierra seca*, or dry land. Viticulture is cheap and simple, enabling the grape farmers to keep their costs relatively low.

Spain's ugly duckling

La Mancha is vital to the Spanish wine and spirits industry. It is the great region of the Airén grape, a variety whose greatest attribute is that it makes wines that are neutral in character. They are in great demand for blending, and huge quantities make their way into the blending vats of other regions, increasing the quantity of the base wine without altering its character. Their low cost makes them ideal for distillation, and the region's great distilleries, many of them in the town of Tomelloso, produce the life blood of Spain's spirit industries (gin and *aguardiente*) as well as the great brandy houses of Jerez. The region may be regarded as Spain's ugly duckling. But other regions are more dependent on it than they would care to admit.

New developments

Unfortunately, this cannot disguise the fact that La Mancha is one of the most backward regions of Spain. Selling cheap wine does not generate big profits for re-investment, and

much of its production plant is obsolete. The Airén, therefore, is frequently overpressed and fermented at a high temperature. The result is a bland, lifeless wine that can be unpleasantly sour.

There is room for optimism, however. With outside investment, some local firms have built new wineries that are amongst the most modern in Spain, and are producing good, cold-fermented light whites, that are intended to be drunk while young. While the planting of more red varieties (there are even plantings of Cabernet Sauvignon, although its use has not yet been authorized) and the importation of more oak barrels for ageing has led to the production of small quantities of some interesting reds. This handful of progressive firms still accounts for only a small percentage of the region's total production, and they have not led the region into a new wine age yet, but a start has certainly been made.

Valdepeñas

Standing like a proud enclave at the southern edge of the *meseta*, Valdepeñas is a smaller region, and very different in character. It has the same climate as La Mancha, giving it the benefit of low-cost production.

But it is more compact, and demand for its wines from Madrid has been strong since the 16th century. These years of steady commerce with the capital city have enabled it to invest continuously in new technology, leaving it well ahead of its giant neighbour.

Traditionally, it has been known for its *claretes*, or light fruity and refreshing reds made from a blend of the Airén and the Cencibel (the Tempranillo), often served in jugs in the restaurants of Madrid and the South. But it also produces a small amount of white wine which, with the aid of its advanced stainless steel crushers and fermentation tanks, is of a good general standard, though not exciting. Furthermore, as the number of oak barrels has increased so too has its production of oak-aged *crianzas* and *reservas*. Silkily smooth, with a deep colour, good fruit and subtle touches of oak, these are good enough to compete with the best in Spain. When their price is taken into consideration, they are, without doubt, some of the best buys available in the country.

The barrels below belong to Rodriguez and Berger, one of the leading wine companies of La Mancha. Unfortunately, the winery in Cinco Casas is not open to the public.

Madrid, Aranjuez, Toledo

The cafés of the Plaza Mayor in Madrid are a popular haunt of tourists and Madrileños.

Madrid has always vied with Barcelona for the distinction of being Spain's most lively, vibrant city. But there is one great difference: close to the border with France, Barcelona is a cosmopolitan city. Madrid, almost in the exact centre of the peninsula, has remained Spanish to its very fingertips.

Bars and restaurants

There can be few cities in the world that rival Madrid for its sheer wealth and variety of places to eat and drink. At one end of the scale, it has some of the most sophisticated restaurants in the world. At the other it has innumerable unpretentious bars offering a bewildering array of *tapas* (see page 96) that are served with drinks. You can start the evening on the terrace of one of the bars in the lovely, enclosed Plaza Mayor, and then walk towards the maze of small streets to the South of the Puerta del Sol, where you will be spoilt for a choice of restaurant.

The traditional cafés

Perhaps the most fascinating establishments that the city has to offer, however, are the traditional cafés. Good examples are the Café Comercial on the Plaza de Bilbao, the León on the Calle de Alcala and the Gijón on the Paseo de Recoletos, the last two conveniently close to the

MADRID
Recommended wine shops:
Try the wine departments in any branch of the Corte Inglés department stores.

Recommended restaurants:
El Botín Cuchilleros 17. Tel: 266 42 17. Book in advance. Traditional Castilian roast meats. Central.
Casa Paco Puerta Cerrada II. Tel: 266 31 66. Old and traditional. Central position.
Jockey Amador de los Rios 6. Tel: 419 10 03. Sophisticated, and expensive.
La Trucha Manuel Fernández y Gonzalez 3. Tel: 231 90 32. Typically Castilian, good *tapas*. Central.

Prado – the home of one of the world's most famous collections of fine art.

Aranjuez
From Madrid the wide NIV leads south to Aranjuez, a drive of about 40km (25 miles).

Aranjuez has often been described as an oasis in the great dusty and dry *meseta* of New Castile. Initially its royal palaces were built as a refuge from the searing heat of the Madrid summer. Its fabulous gardens, the inspiration of the guitarist-composer Rodrigo's *Concierto de Aranjuez*, and of the paintings of the Catalan artist Santiago Rusiñol (1861–1931), are its chief attraction. And you can have a splendid lunch at La Rana Verde (Green Frog) on the Tagus banks.

Toledo
Just a few kilometres beyond Aranjuez the N400 branches westwards to Toledo. The city lacks special gastronomic interest, although there are some reasonable bars and restaurants near the Plaza de la Magdalena. But no one should miss the opportunity to see it.

Toledo is famous for its superb metalwork, especially swords; it has a great artistic heritage (the painter El Greco lived here from 1577 until his death in 1604); and it has an incomparable position, with its impressive Alcázar standing on the rock, flanked on three sides by the river Tagus. Few other cities in Spain, even in Europe, can offer so much. The city stands out like a jewel in the desolate plain.

La Mancha

The best time of the year to visit La Mancha is during October. By then the burning heat of the summer will be beginning to die down. It is the time of the wine harvest, and the time when the *Crocus sativus* comes into bloom, covering the ochre plains to the South of Toledo with what looks like a mauve carpet.

The 'Gold of La Mancha'
Introduced to Spain by the Moors, the *Crocus sativus* yields one of the world's most expensive spices: the golden saffron, the spice that makes the *paella* such a brilliant dish. It is planted in other countries of the Mediterranean, but this western part of La Mancha around the town of Consuegra is the greatest source.

The famous Jardin del Principe in Aranjuez (see page 67) was originally landscaped for Charles IV in the 18th century.

Consuegra is 70km (43 miles) to the South of Toledo along the C400 and, during most of the year, it is a rather drab place. Once a year, however, on the last Sunday of October, known as the 'Día de la Rosa del Azafrán' or Saffron Rose Day, it blossoms into a colourful fiesta. An elected Dulcinea de la Mancha presides over a joyful celebration of singing and dancing, and the local girls traditionally display the jewellery that they have bought with their earnings from the harvest work.

Into the wine country
From Consuegra it is a short hop of 20km (12 miles) to Puerto Lápice on the NIV. This is another typically

The phrase 'un lugar de La Mancha' (a place in La Mancha) along with the silhouetted figures of the old Don and his horse Rosinante evoke the classic Spanish masterpiece by Cervantes, Don Quijote. Herencia is one of many towns associated with episodes in Don Quijote's story.

Manchegan town and has the best and most picturesque restaurant of the region, the Venta el Quijote. For lovers of literature it is also here that Don Quijote (Quixote) was supposed to have been knighted by the innkeeper.

From Puerto Lápice it is a short drive to Alcázar de San Juan, a congenial town in which to stop overnight.

El Toboso and Mota del Cuervo

From Alcázar, you can make a day trip that combines places of literary and vinous interest. Take the N420 that leads eastwards to Mota del Cuervo and, at the town of Pedro Muñoz 20km (12 miles) away, take the turn-off to El Toboso. This is a charming, unspoilt Manchegan town where Quijote discovered his damsel, Dulcinea. The Dulcinea House is worth visiting. Then return to the main road and follow it up to Mota del Cuervo, a town dominated by a row of windmills. If you are

lucky you will be able to visit the great wine co-operative of Nuestra Señora de Manjavacas. This is by no means the largest winery in the region but, with its endless halls of *tinajas* (huge earthenware jars for fermenting and storing wine), it is very typical and makes wines that are well above average.

MOTA DEL CUERVO
Co-operativa Nuestra Señora de Manjavacas
Felix Palacios 14, Mota del Cuervo. Tel: 18 00 25/18 05 63 (Manuel Bobillo). Mon-Fri, 0900–1330, 1600–1800. TP. WS. T.

PUERTO LAPICE
Recommended restaurant:
Venta El Quijote Puerto Lápice. Tel: 57 61 00. Typical Castilian.

ALMAGRO
Recommended hotel:
Parador Nacional Ronda
de San Francisco,
Almagro. Tel: 86 01 00.

MANZANARES
Co-operativa del Campo
Nuestro Padre Jesús del
Perdón Zona Industrial
del Polígono, Manzanares.
Tel: 61 03 09 (Miguel
Garcia). Mon-Fri
0900–1400, 1600–1900. TF.
WS. E. T.

Recommended hotel:
Parador Nacional C,tra
Madrid-Cádiz Km 173.
Tel: 61 04 00.

VILLARROBLEDO
Bodegas Fermín Ayuso
Roig Villarrobledo. Tel:
14 04 58 (Sñr Ayuso). Mon-
Fri 0900–1400, 1600–1900.
TF. WS. E. T.

From Mota take the N301 in the
direction of Albacete and, after 30km
(19 miles), branch off southwards to
Villarrobledo. This is the home of
one of the best privately-owned firms
of the region, Bodegas Ayuso, which
produces excellent oak-aged reds.
Then return back to Alcázar de San
Juan via Tomelloso.

Manzanares and Almagro
Manzanares is 45km (28 miles) from
Alcázar. It is a smaller town but still
an important agricultural centre and
it has two leading wineries. First is
Vinicola de Castilla, a modern
company with perhaps the most
advanced production facilities in
Spain, which produces some
interesting reds. Second is another
giant co-operative, the Co-operativa
Nuestro Padre Jesús del Perdón. This

*These windmills, the legendary giants of Don
Quijote's story, stand in the town of Campo de
Criptana, between Alcázar and Mota.*

firm is best known for its whites
under the Casa la Teja or Yuntero
brands, some of which are released
while young, and others that are
given a year's ageing in tank. They
have an impressive seal of approval:
they are said to be among the
favourites of the King of Spain.

From Manzanares, a small and
rough road leads to Almagro. This
is not a wine town, but its Plaza
Mayor is one of the most interesting
squares in the region. On its south
side is the Corral de Comedias,
where some of the earliest Spanish
plays were performed.

Almagro also has an excellent
Parador; otherwise the C415 leads to
Valdepeñas.

Valdepeñas

Old men pass the time of day in the peaceful central square of Almagro.

The town of Valdepeñas lies just off the NIV, 25km (16 miles) from Manzanares and 70km (44 miles) from Alcázar de San Juan. Its centre, the Plaza de España, has a nice Gothic church, a shaded arcade and some colourful houses. Apart from the bodegas and cheese firms and the usual bustle of a busy agricultural town, this is about all that it has to offer.

The wine town

Valdepeñas is, however, a real wine town. For its population of no more than 30,000 people it has some 350 wine companies; it even has an avenue dedicated to wine, the Avenida del Vino, which is lined with *tinajas*, the huge amphora-shaped jars in which the wine was traditionally fermented and stored.

The wine train

Wine-making has been the town's livelihood for several centuries. By the first half of the 17th century, it had established itself as the chief wine supplier to Madrid, a position that was consolidated first by the building of the Camino Real, the road linking Madrid and Andalusia, and then by the railway that followed the same route. Completed in 1861, the railway soon carried one wine train a day to the capital, consisting of 40 wagons, and known as the *tren del vino*.

This lucrative flow of trade laid the town's strong economic foundations and enabled it to survive two great tragic events.

VALDEPENAS
Bodegas Félix Solís S.A. Ctra Madrid-Cádiz Km 199, Valdepeñas. Tel: 32 34 00 (Sñrta Maria del Mar Moya). Mon-Fri 0800–1400, 1600–1900, Sat 0800–1300. TF. WS. E. T.
Co-operativa La Invencible Raimundo Caro Paton 102, Valdepeñas. Tel: 32 27 77. Mon-Fri 0900–1300, 1500–1900. TF. WS. T.
Recommended restaurants:
La Aguzadera Ctra Andalusia Km 197, Valdepeñas. Tel: 32 32 08.
Casa El Cojo Clle Balbuena, near the Plaza de España, Valdepeñas. Famous tavern.
El Hidalgo Ctra Andalusia Km 194, Valdepeñas. Tel: 32 32 50.

Disaster and progress

During the Napoleonic invasion Valdepeñas was ransacked by the French. Then, at the beginning of the 20th century, the region was laid to waste by phylloxera. So much wine was already in store, however, that its traders managed to continue their business while the vineyards were replanted. Today it is still a prosperous area. Its producers have kept up with production technology and the leading wineries are amongst the most modern in Spain.

The wines

While La Mancha is on the wide open plain, Valdepeñas is virtually in a valley (its name is derived from *valle de piedras* or valley of stones) formed by three Sierras, the Sierras Prieto, del Peral and del Cristo. Rising to over 300m (1,000 ft), these protect the region from the sea's warm breezes, and it suffers from the same extremes of temperature as the open *meseta*. In this climate the Cencibel grape thrives, producing wines with greater acidity than in the North and, importantly, with more colour. Even when blended with more white than red this colour keeps its strength. This helps to explain the region's great paradox: Valdepeñas is primarily a red wine region but some 85 per cent of its vineyard area is covered by the popular white Airén.

A computer panel controls the flows of wine and must in Vinícola de Castilla, one of Spain's most advanced wineries, and a model of Castile's new technology.

Reds and *claretes*

Traditionally, the region's famous *claretes* were made from a mixture of red and white wine. Today, however, the white must is left in contact with red grapes for colour extraction and the process produces wines that are darker than rosés, intensely fruity and refreshing enough to quench the strongest summer thirst.

In an effort to break the dominance of the Airén, the Consejo has decreed that only the Cencibel can now be planted. Production of *crianzas* and *reservas* made entirely from this grape and aged for a year or two is, therefore, on the increase, and they are wonderful value.

The bodegas

In contrast to La Mancha, Valdepeñas is compact and most of its wineries are in the town itself. Amongst the most modern are Luis Megía and Bodegas los Llanos on the outskirts of the town. Then there is the Co-operativa La Invencible (open to visitors), the largest co-operative of the Denomination and one which produces about 30 per cent of its wine. Finally there is the more picturesque family-owned Bodegas Félix Solis in the centre which is also open to visitors (it also has modern equipment).

Manchego cheese

Valdepeñas is one of the largest centres of traditional Manchegan cheese-making in the country, and its production is now strictly controlled by the government. For example, it must be made from sheep's milk produced in La Mancha's four provinces, and it comes in three different styles: *fresco* (fresh), matured for the minimum of 60 days; *curado*
(cured), matured for a minimum of 13 weeks; and *añejo* (aged), matured for a minimum of seven months. The result is a flavoursome, firm, round cheese of about 2.5 kilos. And it goes excellently with the local wine.

Further travel

From Valdepeñas, the wine tour heads towards the great fortified wine regions of the South. The NIV continues down through the impressive Despeñaperros gorge on the border of Andalusia to the town of Bailén with its Parador and then swings westwards to Córdoba which is about 180km (112 miles) away.

Huge steel tanks store the wine at Félix Solís, one of the largest and best-known wine companies in Valdepeñas.

Food and Festivals

FOODS FROM NEW CASTILE

La Mancha's cuisine is not the most imaginative in the country. But, in good restaurants, it can be very tasty and warming.

Dishes from Madrid
The Madrileños love wining and dining. So it is little wonder that they have developed their own special recipes, some of which have become famous throughout Spain.

Perhaps the two most famous of these are the delicious *Callos a la Madrileña* which is served either as a main course or as a *tapa* and consists of tripe stewed with veal, *chorizo* and *morcilla*, onions and paprika; and *Cocido Madrileño*, another stew made with a mixture of meats (such as beef, chicken or veal), sausages (*chorizo* and *morcilla* again), chickpeas and vegetables such as carrots, cabbage and potatoes. Traditionally, this was served as a three-course meal of soup, vegetables and meat rather like the Catalan *Escudella i Carn d'Olla*.

Dishes from La Mancha
It is said that Philip II established Madrid as the capital of the country because it was a convenient place for

PLAZA DE TOROS

SOMBRA

TAQUILLAS

his hunting parties to gather, and small game is certainly abundant on the great *meseta* of La Mancha. Partridges are particularly popular around Toledo and form the basis of the famous *Perdices a la Toledana* where they are cooked in a pot with potatoes, garlic and wine. Elsewhere, game is usually incorporated into the region's famous stews which were made with whatever the shepherds had to hand. The most famous of these is the very popular *Gazpacho Manchego* (see page 130), which can also be found in the Levante.

Sheep are also plentiful in La Mancha, wandering the endless plains in large flocks. Their milk is used to make the famous Manchegan cheese (see page 73), but roast lamb is also a popular dish.

Vegetable dishes
Finally, New Castile has two famous vegetable dishes, *Judías Verdes a la Española* and *Pisto Manchego*. The first is a simple dish of green beans cooked in tomato sauce with onions, garlic, spices and slivers of ham, while the second has often been compared to the French ratatouille, made with onions, courgettes, tomatoes and peppers and often including slices of ham or chicken.

*The Plaza de Toros, the bullring of the small but lively town of Alcázar de San Juan, has a grand entrance. Spectators choose between seats in the sun (*sol*) or shade (*sombra*).*

75

Andalusia

**Jerez-Xérès-Sherry
Manzanilla-Sanlúcar de Barrameda**

**MONTILLA
MORILES**

or many people, Andalusia embodies the image that modern Spain is trying to leave behind: bullfighting, flamenco, cheap seaside resorts, Sangría and so on. But the moment you leave the Costa del Sol, there is something magical about this great, sprawling southern region. If you can avoid the tourist traps, motoring around Andalusia can be a truly memorable experience.

It can also, however, be an arduous one. It is *the* region in Spain for *vinos generosos* or fortified wines: these, with the olive oil of the cuisine, can give head and liver a severe pounding. Furthermore, the province's three main wine regions are far apart and often linked by poor roads that make driving difficult; and temperatures in the summer, particularly on the open road, can become debilitatingly high.

From Valdepeñas in New Castile, the suggested route continues south along the NIV to the small town of Bailén, and then swings westwards to Córdoba. The wine country of Montilla lies to the South of Córdoba, and is reached by leaving the NIV and turning off on the N331, which leads to Montilla.

From here, the N331 continues south to Antequera and joins the N321 just to the South of the town. This excellent dual carriageway descends quickly to Málaga.

Leaving Málaga, you are faced with two alternatives. The easiest way to the 'Sherry Triangle' is along the coastal N340, which passes such famous (or notorious) towns as Torremolinos and Marbella. For a more scenic route, the C344 branches off from the N340 between the airport and Torremolinos, and leads to Ronda via Alhaurin el Grande and Coín. This is tough driving, particularly in the summer, but the beauty of Ronda and the hilltop town of Arcos de la Frontera makes it worthwhile. From Arcos, it is a short drive along the N342 to Jerez.

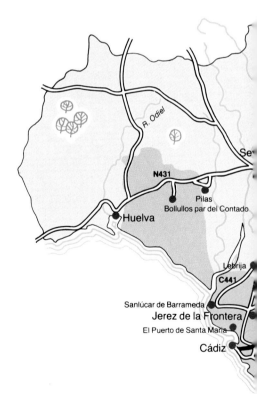

Condado de Huelva

Montilla-Moriles

Jerez-Manzanilla-Sanlúcar

Málaga

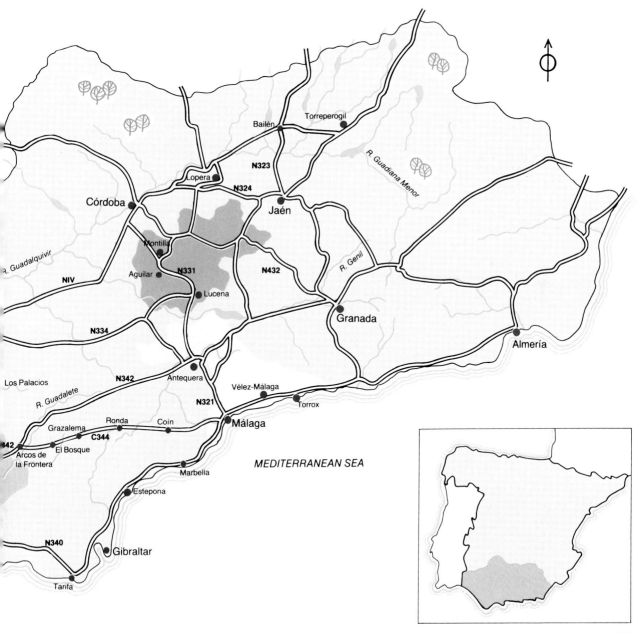

Córdoba

The Denomination Montilla-Moriles embraces some 16,000 hectares of vineyard; of these some 2,700 of *albariza* or *albero* soil have been designated as a *Zona Superior*, which usually produces dry or Fino wines. The *arenas* or *ruedo* soils, composed mostly of sand with clay and limestone, usually make heavier wines or Olorosos. Finos are normally made from the free-run must, or that of the first pressing, while the Olorosos are made from that of the second.

The Pedro Ximénez is the principal grape variety with smaller quantities of Layrén (Airén), Baladí and Torrontés.

CORDOBA
Recommended restaurant:
El Caballo Rojo Cardenal Herrero 28, Córdoba. Tel: 22 38 04. Sophisticated Andalusian food.

MONTILLA
Alvear S.A. Maria Auxiliadora 1, 145000 Montilla. Tel: 65 01 00 (Luis Jimenez or Francisco Segura). Mon-Fri 1000–1600 (May 15–Sep 1); 1000–1300, 1530–1730 (rest of year). TF. WS.
Tomás Garcia S.A. Llano de Palacio 7, Montilla. Tel: 65 02 35/65 07 86 (Enrique Martinez or Manuel Alcaide). Mon-Fri 0900–1300. Closed Aug. TF. WS. T. (This is an associated company of Carbonell. Ask here for details on visiting the winery in Aguilar de la Frontera.)

The first stop of your Andalusian tour is the justly famous city of Córdoba. Once the centre of a powerful Moorish Caliphate and the capital of the Roman province of Baetica, it has numerous monuments belonging to its historic past: on its outskirts are the ruins of the Medina Azahara Palace built by the Moors in the 10th century; in the centre stands the Alcázar, a solid fort with splendid gardens; a sturdy Roman bridge crosses the muddy Guadalquivir; and, of course, there is the great Mezquita Mosque. With the possible exceptions of Granada and Seville, one could not hope for a better introduction to this great southern province.

The Judería of Córdoba
For the wine and food enthusiast there is an added bonus here. The old Jewish quarter or Judería is a maze of small alleys between whitewashed houses. Once a year, during May, this district bursts into bloom during the 'Festival de los Patios Córdobeses', when the inhabitants dress their courtyards, balconies and squares in flowers. For the rest of the year, the colour is provided by a wealth of small, hidden bars and restaurants where chilled Montilla is served with a wide variety of *tapas*. An evening spent prowling these alleys from bar to bar can be a thoroughly enjoyable experience, however much one may regret it the next day! For the more sophisticated, there is the famous Caballo Rojo restaurant which serves a wonderful range of local dishes.

The sherry connection
Córdoba's great wine is Montilla, produced just to the South of the city

in the wine towns of Montilla itself, Moriles and Aguilar de la Frontera. To many it is very similar to sherry: and it is this resemblance that has been the producers' greatest headache in recent years.

Up until 1944, when the Denomination was first established,

much of the region's wine was sold to the great sherry houses of Jerez where it was, quite legally, pumped into their *solera* systems (for a fuller explanation see page 88), and eventually sold as sherry. Since then, however, this practice has been made illegal and the Montilla producers

have had to stand on their own feet. Dispelling the myth that their wines are a cheap alternative to sherry has been an arduous task. But they have invested wisely, raised the quality of their wines and established a following among drinkers who prefer their lower strength.

The Mezquita of Córdoba is a Moorish mosque dating back to the 8th century, during the period of Moorish occupation in southern Spain. Along with the Alhambra at Granada, this is one of the great examples of Moorish architecture in Spain.

Montilla

The butts of Montilla in the Alvear bodegas (see facing page) are placed one on top of another in the traditional solera system (see page 88). The soleras are at ground level with the criaderas above them.

Montilla styles
There are two basic types of Montilla, both of which are dry: the pale, light Fino, and the darker, fuller-bodied Oloroso. The addition of varying amounts of sweetening wine, however, has enabled the Montillans to produce a wider range of styles, like sherry styles (see pages 86–87):
Fino (Pale Dry) Pale in colour and dry.
Amontillado (Medium) A Fino that has been left in cask until its colour has turned to amber. Dry but fuller-bodied than a Fino.
Pale Cream A Fino that has been sweetened. Golden in colour.
Palo Cortado Between a Fino and an Oloroso. Very rare.
Oloroso Brown in colour, full-bodied, pungent, dry.
Cream An Oloroso that has been sweetened. Dark and richly sweet.
Pedro Ximénez Made from grapes that have been dried in the sun. Raisiny, almost black and extremely sweet.
Alcohol in all these styles ranges from around 14 to 22 per cent.
It must be noted that, in the U.K., the terms Fino and Amontillado are reserved for sherry only: Pale Dry and Medium are used for the same styles of Montilla.

Sherry and Montilla
There are a number of similarities between these wines. Both have a basic range of styles – Fino, Amontillado, Oloroso and Cream. And, despite some subtle differences, their production process is generally the same.
In Montilla, after the wine's first fermentation, it is transferred into *tinajas*, the earthenware containers with pointed bottoms which are stuck into the cool earth. After the second fermentation, the *flor* begins to develop, a thick layer of yeasts that covers the mouth of the *tinaja*. The *flor* enables the wine-maker to classify the wines (see also page 88). Then, after two years in butt, the wine is put through the *solera* process, a system that the Montillans claim that they invented.

The differences
Despite all of this, however, sherry and Montilla have important differences. Few people would claim that Montilla can achieve the intensity and complexity of a good sherry, and dry Montilla is never as dry as a Jerez Fino, let alone a Manzanilla. But the most important difference is the result of climate and the grape varieties used.
While the great grape of Jerez is the Palomino, in Montilla it is the Pedro Ximénez; after the blistering heat of the Córdoban summer, this variety produces wines with a high alcoholic strength. Herein lies the crucial difference: while sherry is always fortified, dry Montilla never is and Oloroso only when it has insufficient natural strength. As a result, Montilla is usually lighter.

The wine country
The small town of Montilla is a mere 45km (28 miles) from Córdoba along the N4 and then the smaller C331 which winds its way through the countryside. Around the town, the vineyards can be seen planted on the famous *albariza*, a soil that has a high chalk content; it is grey-white in colour with yellow streaks and produces the best wines.
The town itself is typically Andalusian with the wilting heat of the sun reflected from the white walls of the houses, and colourful flower pots hung from the windows and balconies. Although the traveller is advised to stay in Córdoba (see page 78), Montilla has a reasonable hotel with a small swimming pool; and there is an excellent restaurant, Las Camachas, on its outskirts, shaded by big trees and built around interior courtyards with murmuring fountains. It is also the home of three of the largest and most important companies of the Denomination.

Conde de la Cortina (above) is one of Alvear's most famous brands of Montilla. Another famous Montilla producer, Carbonell, has built a new winery along the traditional lines at Aguilar de la Frontera, near Montilla (below).

The bodegas

The principal of these is the old firm of Alvear founded in 1842 and now the giant of the region. Although its winery in Montilla is only used for ageing purposes, it is set in large, well-kept gardens, and with its long dark buildings full of old barrels, it is a very beautiful winery indeed. Also in the centre is the equally attractive Bodegas Pérez Barquero, more of a working winery with its long rows of earthenware *tinajas*. Bodegas Montulia, despite the prestige of its wines, is rather run down.

The most beautiful Bodega is that of Carbonell in nearby Aguilar de la Frontera, a few kilometres away. Owned by one of the leading olive oil companies of Spain, it is comparatively modern but has been built in the traditional Andalusian style, with its great ageing hall built along the lines of the Mezquita. It is a quiet and beautiful place.

Recommended restaurant:
Las Camachas Ctra Córdoba-Málaga. Tel: 65 00 04.

Málaga

The castle at Antequera has wonderful gardens.

The Denomination of Málaga covers some 16,000 hectares of vineyard, although only about 3,000 of these are used for wine grapes. In general these can be divided into two main areas: the Axarquía, near the coast around the towns of Velez Málaga and the city itself; and the higher ground of the Antequera plain. The first is planted mostly with Moscatel, the second with Pedro Ximénez.

Málaga styles

Málaga comes in several styles which vary from the dry to the intensely sweet. The level of alcohol varies too but is usually 15 to 18 per cent. The main styles are:

Seco Amber in colour, full-bodied but fermented to dryness. A comparatively new style.

Lágrima Made from the free-run juice of the grapes; dark, intense and sweet.

Pedro Ximénez Made from the grape of that name, usually darker than the Moscatel; sweet.

Moscatel Usually golden in colour. Ranging from very sweet to relatively dry.

Solera Smooth, often almost black in colour. Very intense and sweet.

From Montilla the N331 leads in a southerly direction across the very heart of Andalusia. This is a good, modern road and from it you can appreciate the full majesty of the landscape of this southern province with its pale, rolling hills criss-crossed by the precise lines of the olive groves.

Antequera, some 60km (38 miles) from Montilla is worth a short stop. Although it was soon retaken, its mighty castle was the first Moorish stronghold to fall to the Christians when they launched their final offensive against the kingdom of Granada in 1410. From its battlements, there is a glorious view over the great plain of Antequera which lies 500m (1,800 ft) above sea level, and where most of the vineyards used in the production of Málaga wine are planted. Then it is on to the N321, and a slow descent down the southern slopes of the western Sierra de Almijara to the city of Málaga.

The city

As most tourists who land at its airport do not even bother to visit it, Málaga is still a very unspoilt Spanish city. Near the port are some splendid gardens and tree-lined avenues overlooked by the great Alcazaba fortress.

Málaga is a lively, congenial place, and it is best visited at Eastertime when there are magnificent religious processions (if you have not already chosen to go to the bigger, more famous celebrations in Seville). The Spanish Foreign Legion at Málaga also holds a parade near the port. In the eastern part of the city is the district of El Palo with some excellent restaurants on the beach that serve fish caught the same day in the bay. To the West the Costa del Sol, with its discotheques and hotels, stretches uninterrupted as far as Gibraltar.

Málaga's vineyards

One of the few benefits to have come out of the phylloxera disaster is that most of the vineyards planted near the coast, which were unsuitable for grape-growing, have been abandoned. Today, therefore, most of the grapes come from higher, cooler vineyards. Furthermore, the varieties used in wine production have been rationalized from the 30 used before phylloxera to just two: the Pedro Ximénez, planted in the higher areas, and the Moscatel planted lower down in the coastal regions east of Málaga.

The crushing and fermentation of the must is usually carried out in small, rustic wineries near the vineyards and then, by law, the wine has to be transported to the city where a more stable climate is better for ageing. All wines must be aged for a minimum of two years in wood: some are just left in the same barrel; others, the real aristocrats, are put through the *solera* system (see page 88), which makes them smooth, more concentrated and intense.

López Hermanos S.A.
Clle Canadá 10, Polígono Industrial El Viso, 29080 Málaga. Tel: 33 03 00. (Bruce Miller or Sñrta Maria-Teresa Diaz). Mon-Fri 0900–1400. Closed Aug. TF. WS. E. T. (See page 84.)

Scholtz Hermanos S.A.
Ctra Cádiz Km 238,500. Tel: 31 36 02/07 (Pedro Ankersmit). Mon-Fri 0800–1500, Sat 0800–1330. Closed Aug. TF. WS. E. T. (See page 84).

The rolling hills of the Andalusian interior have a strangely lunar quality. This is the homeland of the fortified wines of the South.

From Málaga to Jerez

The magnificent cliffs at Ronda hide a grisly secret – a mass execution took place here in the 1930s. Hemingway's novel For Whom the Bell Tolls *includes a description of the scene, one of many tragedies in the Spanish Civil War.*

Málaga's varieties
Málaga wine comes in several styles, from Málaga Seco, a full-bodied apéritif, to the more traditional sweet dessert wines. At their best these are unctuously smooth wines, with a raisiny aroma and flavour, and an intensity that lingers for long in the mouth.

The bodegas
Unfortunately, there are only two important bodegas left in the city of Málaga. The first is López Hermanos, which is buried away in an industrial estate, but produces a comprehensive range of wines.

The second, Scholtz Hermanos, on the road to the airport, is the producer of Solera 1885, regarded by many as the greatest Málaga of them all. Neither bodega is particularly beautiful, but for lovers of interesting dessert wines, a visit to either is worthwhile.

The road to Jerez
From Málaga the traveller has a choice of two routes to the 'Sherry Triangle': the first follows the coast along the N340 to a junction just before Cádiz, and then continues along the NIV; the second is a more complicated inland route.

The Costas

If beaches and resorts are what you are after, the coastal route is the obvious choice. The N340 takes you along the length of the Costa del Sol and then continues to the quieter Costa de la Luz.

The contrast between the two areas could not be greater. The Costa del Sol is Spain's premier tourist strip, an almost unbroken chain of resorts. In comparison, the Costa de la Luz is unspoilt and undiscovered. Most of its holiday-makers are Spanish, and its long, golden beaches make those of the Costa del Sol look very dull.

The 'Pueblos Blancos'

The alternative route leads through the wild and rugged Serranía de Ronda and passes some picturesque *'Pueblos Blancos'* or white towns, their houses with dazzling white-washed walls, their roofs a colourful jumble of sun-baked tiles.

Leave Málaga on the N340 and, just after the airport, take the windy C344 to the hilltop town of Ronda.

Ronda

Ronda is a wonderful town to visit. It is divided by a dramatic gorge bridged by the impressive Puente Nuevo; its old quarter has an interesting Collegiate church, the Palacio del Marqués de Salvatierra and the oldest bullring in Spain. And delightful gardens, set on the lip of steep cliffs, offer some breathtaking views over the countryside.

Ronda was the scene of a revengeful, hot-blooded mass execution during the Civil War. Hundreds of Nationalists were forced over the edge of the perilous gorge to their deaths, an episode which is vividly described by Hemingway in *For Whom the Bell Tolls*.

Arcos de la Frontera

From Ronda the C344 continues past the pretty town of Grazalema and the National Park of El Bosque to the town of Arcos de la Frontera. Set on a high hill overlooking the Guadalete, the town has some spectacular views, while its maze of small streets and alleyways has numerous handicraft shops. With its Parador on the central square, it is an excellent place to stay the night.

From Arcos the N342 leads directly to Jerez.

WARNING
The N3240 between Málaga and Estepona is known by the locals as the 'Killer Road' and is one of the most dangerous stretches of road in Europe. Each year more people are killed on it than on the whole of the British motorway network – so drive with care.

ARCOS DE LA FRONTERA
Parador Nacional 'Casa del Corregidor' Pl. de España, Arcos del la Frontera. Tel: 70 05 00.

Sherry Styles

Fino

Pale and dry. The lightest and most delicate of the four styles, it varies according to where it is aged. Those from Jerez are usually heavier in body and alcohol than those from Puerto; those of Sanlúcar, nearer the coast, known as **Manzanillas**, develop a distinctive salty taste and are the driest of all. The alcohol content is 15.5 to 17 per cent.

Amontillado

Amber in colour with more body than a Fino. By nature the Amontillados are dry, but the more commercial brands are slightly sweetened.

As with the dark Olorosos, these wines gather in intensity and complexity with age, and have a distinctive nutty flavour. The alcohol content is 16 to 18 per cent.

Oloroso

Dark gold in colour, very aromatic as the name implies (*olor* means aroma, *oloroso* means pungent), full-bodied and dry. Similar in style is the much rarer **Palo Cortado**, usually described as a cross between an Oloroso and an Amontillado, full-bodied but slightly paler in colour. The alcohol content in both is 18 to 20 per cent.

Cream

This is a very British invention: an Oloroso sweetened with Pedro Ximénez wine. Dark, almost mahogany in colour, very smooth and richly sweet. A recent variation is the **Pale Cream**, which is a blend of Pedro Ximénez and Fino to produce a sweet but pale wine. The alcohol content in both is about 18 to 20 per cent.

The D.O. Jerez-Zérèz–Manzanilla–Sanlúcar de Barrameda covers some 19,300 hectares and embraces about 7,000 individual vineyards of varying sizes. The best wines come from the parishes of Aniña, Balbaina and Los Tercios (for Finos); Macharnudo (for Amontillados); Carrascal (for Olorosos); and Miraflores and Torrebreba (for Manzanillas). The best soil is the chalky white *albariza* (see also page 78). Then come the *barros* with about 30 per cent limestone and the *arenas*, sand with about 10 per cent limestone.

The Palomino de Jerez dominates the region and covers about 95 per cent of the vineyard area. Smaller quantities of Pedro Ximénez and Moscatel are also grown for the production of sweet wines. Their grapes are dried on *esparto* or grass mats to concentrate their sugar and produce wines that are often too sweet to drink and are used for blending in the production of various wines such as sweet Amontillados, Creams and Pale Creams.

Copitas are the slim and elegant glasses in which sherry is traditionally served in Spain. They are narrowed at the mouth to hold the aroma.

Sherry and the Solera System

The D.O. 'Brandy de Jerez' was established in 1988. It is also only the third brandy to be given this honour (the other two are Cognac and Armagnac). Strict regulations govern its ageing:

Solera Must be aged for a minimum of six months in butt.

Reserva Must be aged for a minimum of one year in butt.

Gran Reserva Must be aged for a minimum of three years in butt.

In practice, however, ageing periods tend to be longer, with the Gran Reservas often aged for six years or more.

The result of a happy combination of climate, soil, grape variety and the expert hand of man, sherry is Spain's only truly unique wine, produced and aged in the 'Sherry Triangle' formed by the towns of Jerez, Puerto de Santa Maria and Sanlúcar de Barrameda. The Palomino Fino grape thrives in its warm, consistent climate, particularly on the chalky white *albariza* soil and, before fortification, it produces pleasant but not outstanding wine. It is, therefore, sherry's ageing and blending process that makes it unique.

The *flor*

After fermentation the wine is transferred to oak butts that are loosely stoppered and never completely filled, to allow a certain amount of ventilation. Then the *flor* or flower begins to develop and grow. The *flor* is a layer of yeasts that forms on the surface of the wine and prevents oxidization by insulating the wine from the atmosphere. Over a period of six months it dies slowly, leaving the wine clear and ready for classification, which depends on the thickness of the *flor*.

It is another of the peculiarities of sherry that no two butts of wine develop in the same manner. The task of the master taster or *capataz*, is to determine the style into which the wine will develop. Usually the more delicate wines with the thickest *flor* will be classified as Finos or Amontillados, and those with the thinnest will become Olorosos. Once classified, the wines are fortified and then introduced to the *solera*.

The *solera* system

The system's purpose is to produce wines of uniform quality and character. It involves several butts, known as the *soleras* and *criaderas*, usually placed one on top of the other. The wine for further blending and bottling is drawn from the *solera* at ground level. Then an equal quantity of wine is brought down from the first *criadera*, and so on.

Continuity in style and character is ensured by the fact that the young wine comes into contact with a far larger quantity of older wine and assumes its character.

The system has been copied all over the world, yet Spanish sherry remains unique in its subtle flavours, a great contribution to wine culture.

Jerez brandy

'The Jerezanos created art with their wine and made money with their brandy', goes a popular saying. Brandy de Jerez, whose production is controlled by a Consejo Regulador, is very different from the brandy made in other parts of the world. The producers buy their wine in other regions and often distill it on the spot before transporting it to the sherry towns for ageing and blending.

In most other regions brandy is aged by a static process, matured in a single barrel. In Jerez, however, it is put through the *solera* system in a similar way to sherry, a process

known as dynamic ageing. The transfer of brandy from butt to butt ensures that it ages faster and becomes smoother, while the addition of caramel, used in varying amounts by the different houses, gives it greater pungency, colour and depth of flavour. Most of them also have a touch of sweetness, although some are completely dry.

At the popular end of the scale the brandy can be fiery and harsh, but the premium end can offer a fascinating range that varies from the comparatively light in colour and dry to the thicker, darker and sweeter brands.

The bodegas of González Byass and the Collegiate Church, which dates back to the 16th and 17th centuries, are two famous landmarks in Jerez.

The Sherry Country

At harvest time in the 'Sherry Triangle' the vendimiadores *pick grapes in the* albariza *vineyards.*

JEREZ

Pedro Domecq S.A. San Idelfonso 3, Jerez. Tel: 33 18 00. Mon-Fri 1000–1300. Closed first three weeks Aug. TF. WS. E. T.

González Byass S.A. Manuel-Maria González 12, 11407 Jerez. Tel: 34 00 00. Mon-Fri 1000–1300. Closed Aug. TF. WS. E. T. Old tasting room, sherry-drinking mice!

Recommended restaurants:

El Bosque Av. Alcalde Alvaro Domecq, Jerez. 30 33 33. *'Haute cuisine'*.
Tendido 6 Clle Circo 10, Jerez. Tel: 34 48 35. Typically Andalusian.

The province of Cádiz in which the 'Sherry Triangle' lies is famous in Spain. For centuries it has been well known for its fighting bulls, bred on great ranches, and for its horses which are a particular passion of its people. Its fiestas, at which many of Spain's best flamenco dancers and bullfighters gather, are legendary.

Cádiz itself, set on a promontory reaching into the sea, has a splendid historic past, a fine collection of paintings by Murillo, and two cathedrals. But, on the international stage, the province is still best known for its wine. The sherry district itself, the 'Triangle', is between three towns: Sanlúcar de Barrameda to the North, on the Guadalquivir, Jerez de la Frontera further south and east, and Puerto de Santa Maria on the coast, further south again.

Jerez de la Frontera

This is the largest of the three towns that make up the triangle. In fact it is more of a city than a town, with several good churches and other historic buildings. The 16th-century Collegiate Church (near the bodegas of González Byass and Domecq) is particularly attractive, set at the top of a wide flight of stone steps. Jerez also has a Moorish fortress, the Alcázar, dating back to the 12th century. It is also the home of the Andalusian School of Equestrian Art, which holds public displays of superb horsemanship every Thursday.

Its centre has all the hallmarks of a prosperous commercial city: office blocks, the usual mass of Spanish banks, and restaurants packed at lunchtime with smartly dressed executives. Unfortunately, it also suffers from a disease common to most Spanish cities: the encroachment of unattractive suburbs of tall apartment blocks separated by colourless, dusty streets. On the surface therefore, Jerez is no more than a normal but busy city in southern Andalusia.

The vaults of Jerez

As usual, however, appearances are deceptive. For behind high, white-washed walls and wrought-iron gates, there is another, almost secret world. One of long, cool bodegas with high vaulted ceilings and swept earth floors; of rows of dark oak butts with warped faces full of pungent, maturing sherry; of colourful, immaculately kept gardens shaded by tall trees; and of inner patios with tinkling fountains. It is like a hidden city, and one cannot help falling in love with it.

Historic legacies

The exact date of Jerez's foundation is unknown, but it stands in a corner of Andalusia that has benefited from a succession of foreign influences, many of which have left their mark on its towns and the character of its people. Even before the Moorish occupation in AD 711, the area had witnessed the arrival and departure of Phoenicians, Greeks, Carthaginians, Romans, Vandals and the Visigoths. The Moors stayed for five and a half centuries and their influence can be clearly seen in the city's architecture. More recently, the British have established roots.

The British connection

Opinions differ, but it is thought that British merchants began to trade in

the region in the early 14th century, and the trade has been flourishing ever since.

In time, the British merchants established their own companies – Sandeman, Duff Gordon, Osborne, Williams & Humbert, Croft, John Harvey and many more, still wholly or partially British-owned. These companies adapted the product to the tastes of their clients, adding sweetening wine to make up different styles, such as Cream.

A venenciador *demonstrates his skills at the bodegas of Domecq in Jerez. The* venencia *with which he draws samples from the butts is traditionally made of whalebone and silver. Both Domecq and González Byass have displays of barrels signed by famous visitors.*

A glass-bottomed barrel (above) reveals the mystery of the flor *(see page 88). The bull (above right) is the famous symbol of Osborne.*

JEREZ (*continued*)
Garvey S.A. Clle Divinia Pastora 3, 11402 Jerez. Tel: 33 05 00 (Alejandro Diaz). Mon-Fri 1130–1400. Closed Aug. TF. E. T.
John Harvey & Sons (España) Clle Arcos 57, Jerez. Tel: 34 60 00 (Sñrta Macarena Ferguson). Mon-Fri 0900–1400. Closed Aug. TF. WS. E. T. Wine museum, gardens, alligators!
The House of Sandeman Clle Pizarro 10, Jerez. Tel: 30 11 00 (Sñrta Eva Maria Reyes). Mon-Fri 0900–1400. TP. WS.
Williams & Humbert Ltd Nuños de Cañas 1, Jerez. Tel: 33 13 00 (Amaro de la Calle) Mon-Fri 1030–1330. Closed Jul 26–Aug 15. TF. WS. E. T. Gardens, carriages, introductory film.

Great Britain became the biggest market for sherry in the world, bigger even than Spain, a position that it has maintained to this day.

The British connection brought its relics of British culture too: the Polo Club of Jerez, which remains extremely popular, was founded in 1874, a mere four years after the sport was introduced to England from India (Jerez also attracted army officers who were stopping off at Gibraltar on their way to or from India); and even today it is surprising how many Jerezanos have English names.

Bodegas of Jerez
Unfortunately some of Jerez's leading companies – such as the impressive Rancho Croft on the outskirts of the town – are not open to the public. In general, however, the bodegas welcome visitors and have regular conducted tours of their premises which invariably end up with a good-humoured tasting.

The most popular of these tours are of the city's two giants, González

Byass and Pedro Domecq, two firms that personify the sherry industry. Both establishments are almost small towns in their own right, with tree-lined streets separating their numerous bodegas. In González Byass the most notable of these are the Gran Bodega Tio Pepe and the circular La Concha designed by Gustav Eiffel, the great 19th-century engineer. Domecq has the famous El Molino with a collection of ancient barrels signed by such historic figures as the Duke of Wellington, and the Mezquita, built along the lines of the famous mosque in Córdoba. Visits

to these companies are efficiently conducted but they have the disadvantage that you are often shown around in large and boisterous groups. Many travellers may prefer to visit the smaller firms.

Gardens and a museum

If you prefer gardens, then Sandeman and Harveys are the automatic choice, particularly as the latter has a small museum and, of all things, a family of alligators! Otherwise, try the great Bodega San Patricio of Garvey, founded as its name implies by an Irishman in 1780; or the elegant, immaculate Williams & Humbert, possibly the most charming of them all.

Puerto de Santa Maria

Lying on the coast 10km (6 miles) from Jerez is Puerto de Santa Maria. In the past most sherry used to be shipped from the small docks here, but Puerto's southern neighbour, Cádiz, supplanted it in the early part of this century. From the bridge at the mouth of its river there is a fabulous view over the bay to the distant port of Cádiz.

It is much smaller than Jerez, but it is a lively little town with some first class, sophisticated restaurants, and cheaper and more modest alternatives near the railway station. An enjoyable evening can be spent just doing the rounds of its excellent *tapas* bars near the centre which buzz with life at the weekends. There are good beaches on the Atlantic, notably at Valdelagrana, and, for yacht lovers, the brand new Puerto Sherry marina. On its outskirts there is also the best hotel in the area (though it is comparatively expensive), the Caballo Blanco.

Puerto's bodegas

Since it is on the coast, Puerto has a different climate to that of Jerez; it is cooled by the sea breezes and has a higher level of humidity. As a result its dry sherries are slightly different to those reared in Jerez, lighter in alcohol and, some would say, with more finesse and a bigger *flor* aroma.

This is also a great brandy centre, the home of Osborne and Fernando A. de Terry, two of the leading brandy producers in Spain, the latter being as famous for its white Cartujano horses (the breed used at the famous Spanish Riding School in Vienna) as it is for its sherry and brandy. A third large concern based in the town is the family-run firm of Luis Caballero.

It is Osborne and its affiliate Duff Gordon, however, that dominate the town. El Tiro, Osborne's great brandy bodega, is on the left as you enter the town. In the centre of the town it has another major complex which houses its *soleras*, and is open to the public.

PUERTO DE SANTA MARIA
Duff Gordon & Co. and **Osborne y Cia**, Fernán Caballero 2/3, 11500 Puerto de Santa Maria. Tel: 85 52 11 (Tomás Osborne). Mon-Fri 0900–1300. Closed Aug 1–22. TF. WS. E. T. (These companies are associated and are neighbours.)

Recommended restaurants:
Don Peppone Playa Valdelagrana, Puerto de Santa Maria. Tel: 86 10 99. Sophisticated Andalusian food. (For an apéritif beforehand, try some of the sherries at the Bodega Jerezana on the beach front.)
Venta El Corneta On the road from Puerto to Cádiz. Tel: 86 26 15. Typically Andalusian.

A crested, dated barrel at Duff Gordon's San José bodega in Puerto proclaims an illustrious history in fine wines.

Three rare sherries from the family-run firm of Vinícola Hidalgo in Sanlúcar (right, from the top) a Palo Cortado, a Manzanilla and a dry Amontillado.

SANLUCAR
Antonio Barbadillo S.A.
Luis Equilaz 11, Sanlúcar de Barrameda. Tel: 36 02 41 (Sñrta Sarah McWatters). Mon-Fri 0730–1500. TF. WS. E. T.
Vinícola Hidalgo S.A.
Banda de Playa 24, Sanlúcar de Barrameda. Tel: 36 05 16 (Sñrta Lucy Tanner). Mon-Fri 0800–1430. TF. WS. E. T. (Visits depend on staff availability.) The firm is housed in listed buildings.

Recommended restaurants:
All the restaurants on the beach at Sanlúcar can be recommended.
Outstanding are **Bigote** and **Casa Juan**.

Sanlúcar de Barrameda

Sanlúcar, the third sherry town, is at the mouth of the Guadalquivir river, looking across at the Coto de Doñana, one of the largest nature reserves in Europe. It is some 20km (12 miles) from Jerez along a small road that leads through the heart of the region's *albariza* country. It was from this small, dusty town that Columbus sailed on his first great voyage of discovery, a cause of major celebrations here in the 500th

anniversary year, in 1992. Sanlúcar is not a beautiful town, but it has a reasonably priced hotel, and its central square, surrounded by lively bars, is pleasant enough. Down on the river beach is a string of marvellous fish restaurants with an easy, relaxed atmosphere: sitting outside for a meal of lightly fried fish, caught that day, with a bottle of chilled Manzanilla must be one of the greatest pleasure of any tour of Andalusia. In particular look out for the crayfish, said to be the best in all Spain.

Manzanilla

Sanlúcar's other great speciality is Manzanilla. No one is quite sure why this wine is so distinctive, but it is believed that its delicious, salty tang is the result of its ageing by the sea, a theory supported by the fact that, if a butt is taken back to Jerez, it slowly takes on the character of an ordinary Fino. Whatever the reason, Manzanilla is the driest of all sherries, light, delicate and with a splendid bouquet. Also worth looking out for is the rarer Manzanilla Pasada, a wine that has been aged for longer, giving it greater colour and body.

Sanlúcar's bodegas

The town itself is dominated by the giant Antonio Barbadillo, a company that accounts for some 70 per cent of the world's total Manzanilla production. Managed today by the fifth generation of the founding family, the firm dates back to 1821. Its sprawling complex of bodegas, based around a beautiful old Andalusian mansion, occupies most of the upper part of the town. Closer to the centre is the much smaller Vinícola Hidalgo, another family company whose charming, picturesque winery is well worth visiting. A third firm, Delgado Zuleta, also produces notable wines although its winery is, sadly, not open to the public.

Further travel

The 'Sherry Triangle' is where this tour through the centre of Spain ends. But if you want to continue along the wine trail, you are by no means stranded.

Anyone travelling in this region should spend a few days visiting Seville and Granada, two of the most fascinating cities in the country.

Leaving the region from Granada and heading northwards towards the Mediterranean coast, the N342 and the N340 will take you to Murcia and Alicante. The Mediterranean route described in the following two chapters can then be done south to north, reversing the directions given here.

Murcia, incidentally, is a great gastronomic centre, and the home of El Rincón de Pepe, one of the best traditional restaurants in Spain (see page 129).

The inner courtyard of Antonio Barbadillo's old Andalusian mansion lies at the centre of a complex of bodegas which dominates the upper part of Sanlúcar.

Food and Festivals

FOOD SPECIALITIES

Alcachofas a la Montillana Artichoke hearts served in a rich sauce of lemon and Montilla with thin strips of meat.

Estofado de Rabo de Toro Oxtail stew with carrots, peas, onions and fried potatoes.

Gazpacho Andaluz The classic version of this famous dish is also known as *Gazpacho Rojo de Sevilla*, a chilled vegetable soup with tomatoes, peppers, cucumber and garlic, served with fried croutons. Two interesting alternatives are *Ajo Blanco de Málaga*, made with almonds, bread, garlic and grapes, and *Salmorejo de Córdoba*, a thicker version made with tomatoes, bread, garlic and egg yolks.

Huevos a la Flamenca Eggs baked in an earthenware dish with vegetables such as artichokes and broad beans, and *chorizo* and *jamón serrano*.

Migas Andaluzas Breadcrumbs fried in olive oil and flavoured with spices such as cumin, paprika and cloves. In the Alpujarras on the southern slopes of the Sierra Nevada, where this dish is a particular favourite, sardines and green peppers are added and it is served in a large round pan.

Olla Gitana Literally gipsy stew with white beans, bread, pears and an assortment of vegetables including pumpkin and green beans.

Riñónes al Jerez Kidneys with a sauce made from sherry, onions and garlic.

ANDALUSIAN FOOD

In his book *Adventures in Taste*, Don Pohren describes Andalusia as 'a gastronomic desert'. While it is true that one encounters too many restaurants where mediocre dishes are served drenched in olive oil, the food has improved greatly in recent years, making better use of excellent raw materials.

Ham, fish and vegetables

With coasts on the Mediterranean and the Atlantic, the fish – ranging from whitebait and sardines to prawns and lobster – is excellent, and can be best appreciated in the beach restaurants of Málaga and Sanlúcar. Andalusia is also the producer of the best cured ham or *jamón serrano* in Spain, coming from Jabugo, in the province of Huelva and Trevélez in the Sierra Nevada. Its top quality olive oil, almonds and sherry vinegar are already well known. Vegetables, the basis of the famous *Gazpachos*, are increasing in quality and quantity as a result of the great agricultural developments in Almería and the Guadalquivir valley, which will convert this part of Spain into the California of Europe.

Tapas

Perhaps the most charming aspect of Andalusian cuisine are the *tapas*, the small dishes or appetizers served with drinks which can vary from simple plates of olives, peanuts or almonds to more elaborate offerings such as fried squid, prawns, slices of ham or Spanish omelette or *pinchitos*, cubes of spiced meat grilled on a skewer. The perfect accompaniment to a glass of chilled Fino or dry Montilla, these are served in most bars of the South but are the speciality of Seville and Almería, where several of these dishes often make up a meal.

The Caballo Rojo in Córdoba's Judería is one of the city's most famous restaurants (see page 78). Its entrance is discreet and typically Andalusian, with dozens of hanging baskets of geraniums and massed potted plants decorating the whitewashed walls outside.

FESTIVALS

Andalusia is the land of fiestas *par excellence*. Córdoba has its courtyard fair in May (see page 78), Granada its Corpus Christi and the International Festival of Music and Dance (June and July). In Seville, the processions of Holy Week, and the '*Feria de Abril*', with its frenzy of music, dancing and horse parades, are both unforgettable.

Jerez has two annual fairs that celebrate the three things that its people love best: wine, horses, and flamenco dancing and music. The first, the '*Feria del Caballo*', is in May with horse racing, parades and horseback bullfighting. The second is the '*Feria de la Vendimia*' in September, when girls carry the first grapes to be crushed and blessed at the Collegiate Church, doves are released to the sound of ringing bells and a party of drinking and dancing begins. Both are genuinely Spanish affairs, and as yet untouched by commercialism.

Catalonia

PRIORATO

Situated in the north-eastern corner of Spain and looking out over the Mediterranean, Catalonia has always been Spain's most 'European' region. Its historic ties with other parts of Europe are strong, and the Catalans have tended to look more towards Europe than the rest of Spain. They have their own proud cultural heritage, their own language and a sense of their own national identity.

The Catalans are also good businessmen and are said to count even while they dance. Their legendary business acumen and energy have raised their standard of living to the highest in the country and have created a strong industrial base. During this century, this has often been at the expense of agriculture, sucking both capital and labour away from the land. But the wine industry remains important to the economy with six Denominations of Origin producing a wide variety of quality wines, including its unique sparkling wine CAVA.

As the Catalan wine regions are close to the coast, the suggested route is straightforward. From France, drive south – either jumping on and off the A7 or using the tough but more exciting *nacionales* along the coast. If you make a base on the coast you can then make one or two-day trips into the interior.

Southwards from France

The A7 and the N11 cross the border at Le Perthus and lead to Figueras in the heart of the Ampurdán. For more adventurous drivers, the alternative is the windy, coastal Port Bou-Rosas road. From a base there it is a mere 20 to 30-minute drive to the wine country and the best of the wine towns.

To the South, the *autopista* coast road alternative continues. From Rosas the coastal road leads to El Masnou just to the south of Alella. If you take the A7 you should leave it at the Granollers exit and follow the El Masnou signs.

The Penedès and Tarragona

After Barcelona, the Penedès is about an hour's drive on the N340. A base can be made either at Vilafranca or at Sitges, a short drive away. Codorníu's extraordinary Raimat estate is a day trip, near Lérida on the N240 to Huesca and Aragon.

The best bodegas in Tarragona are in the city centre or close to it and, from there, one or two-day excursions can be made to the wine country of the interior. A pleasant alternative is to stay at either Salou or Cambrils.

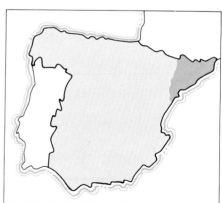

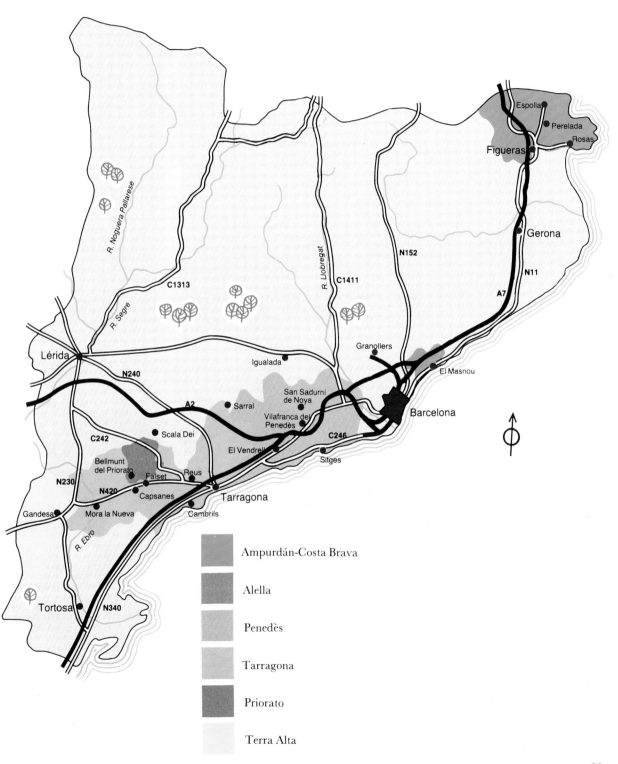

The Wines of Catalonia

Until recently the foreign consumer knew very little about the wines of Catalonia. Together with Rioja, CAVA, the sparkling wine produced mostly in the Penedès by the *méthode champenoise*, is one of the great export successes of the Spanish wine industry. But few people outside Spain realize the quality and variety of wines produced by Catalonia's other Denominations of Origin.

An ancient history

The region's history as a wine producer is a long but chequered one dating back to Phoenician and Greek times. It was during the Roman period that the industry first began to prosper, exporting its wines with such success that further plantings of the vine were banned by Rome to protect its own grape farmers.

This strong foundation was destroyed by centuries of Visigothic and Moorish occupation, and it was not until the 11th century that a long and slow recovery began. The region was united with the rest of Spain in the course of the Middle Ages, with Aragon in 1137 and with Castile in 1497. But it has maintained a strong separatist tradition since then, an independent spirit which has left its stamp on the region's wines.

Cypresses stand guard over a small chapel and cemetery in the midst of vineyards in the Alt Penedès. This is the heartland of Catalonia's most prestigious Denomination.

Catalonia's Golden Age

By the second half of the 18th century, known as the Golden Age of Catalan viticulture, the wine industry had reached a peak of prosperity and importance. Its profits, combined with those of its satellite industries such as cork and glass manufacturing, helped to finance the growth of industry in the region. When the phylloxera destroyed the vineyards of France, the region's economy received one massive final boost that lifted exports to an all-time high and led to the planting of vineyards in virtually every adequate plot of land.

The phylloxera, however, did not stop at the Pyrenees and, by the turn of the century, it had reduced wine exports by half and left numerous grape farmers destitute. Since then there have been periods of expansion, but in general, the vineyard area has decreased steadily. Furthermore, in quality terms, the recovery has been uneven, with the Penedès alone being able to hoist itself to the status of one of Europe's great wine regions. This recovery has only been made possible by the success of CAVA.

The CAVA boom

It was in 1872 that Josep Raventós, the owner of Codorníu, opened the first bottle of Spanish CAVA. The phylloxera arrived some five years later but by then this wine had found a ready market among the prosperous Catalan middle classes. By 1877, Codorníu had replaced Veuve Clicquot as the sparkling wine at royal banquets, and the industry never looked back.

Over the years this boom has generated enough profits to

transform the Penedès into the most technically advanced region in Spain. And it has not been just CAVA that has benefited. With its excellent production facilities and vineyards, the region also produces good 'new style', fresh and crisp whites and smaller quantities of high-quality reds.

A region of variety

Not all of Catalonia, however, has been so successful. Good wines are produced in every region, but outside the Penedès the standard is still often hampered by a lack of investment.

Nevertheless, Catalonia remains an important and varied wine-producing region: it produces CAVA; it produces excellent light whites in the Penedès and Alella; lovely rosés in the Ampurdán; strong and characterful reds in the Priorato; and wonderful *generosos* in Tarragona.

All bottles of CAVA must have the word CAVA prominently displayed on the label along with the words méthode champenoise. *The CAVA cork has a distinctive four-pointed star on its base.*

There are six Denominations of Origin in Catalonia: Ampurdán-Costa Brava and Alella in the North; the Penedès in the centre; and Tarragona, the Priorato and Terra Alta in the South. Between them they cover some 93,400 hectares. There are two further regions, the Costers del Segre in Lérida and the Conca de Barbera, that may soon be elevated to the same status.

By law CAVA can be produced in regions other than Catalonia, namely Navarra, the Rioja and Aragon. The four Catalan provinces, however, account for some 99.5 per cent of the total and the Penedès alone for some 99 per cent.

The Ampurdán and Alella

The 5,800 hectares embraced by the Ampurdán-Costa Brava Denomination are the most northerly in Spain, and are planted primarily with the Garnacha and the Cariñena grapes, with smaller plots of white Macabeo and Xarel.lo. Some imported varieties have also been planted recently but these are still on an experimental basis only.

Some 70 per cent of the region's production is of rosés. Light in alcohol, with a pretty pink colour, they have plenty of fruit and should be drunk young, as should the whites. The region also produces some more sophisticated oak-aged reds and some excellent CAVA.

Perhaps the most interesting wine, however, is the fortified sweet dessert wine, the Garnatxa d'Empordà. With an alcoholic strength of 15 per cent, this wine is often brown in colour due to its ageing in wood and has a rich, raisiny sweetness that is drier and less cloying than a Moscatel, for which it could well be mistaken.

Some firms have also recently launched a *vi de l'any*: a wine released in December following the harvest, with no ageing, in the style of Beaujolais Nouveau.

The wines of Alella

The next Denomination down the coast is the tiny one of Alella covering a mere 380 to 400 hectares. It produces small quantities of light reds and rosés from the Garnacha and the Ull de Llebre (the Tempranillo of the Rioja), but most of its production is of white wines; the traditional barrel-aged semi-sweets and the 'modern', light and young wines made principally from the Pansa Blanca and the Xarel.lo. In recent years the imported Chenin

Blanc and particularly the Chardonnay have been introduced with immense success by Parxet, one of the two companies of the region, and their planting has now been permitted by the Consejo. Parxet also produces some excellent CAVA.

The Ampurdán

The Denomination of Ampurdán-Costa Brava, which lies immediately to the South of the French border, is one of the oldest wine-producing areas in the country. It is believed that the vine was first introduced in the 5th century BC; the industry flowered during the Roman period around the colonies of Rosas and Ampurias, and later under the ecclesiastical orders in the Middle Ages. During the Golden Age of the Catalan vine, it reached a peak of prosperity when its wines were served at the French court. Then the phylloxera dealt it a body blow from which it has never recovered.

Today there is still plenty of evidence of this former glory. If you take the steep and windy road from Rosas to Cadaqués on the Cap de Creus promontory, you can still see the remains of the carefully constructed terraces on which the vines were planted. Its vineyards reached down to the coast and some, so the locals will tell you, were so inaccessible that they had to be harvested from the sea and the grapes transported by boat.

Today the Denomination is very much smaller than it used to be, but it produces good if not outstanding wines. It is also a proud little industry as the carefully tended vineyards of the Alt Empordà or High Ampurdán between the Pyrenees and the Montgris mountains

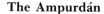

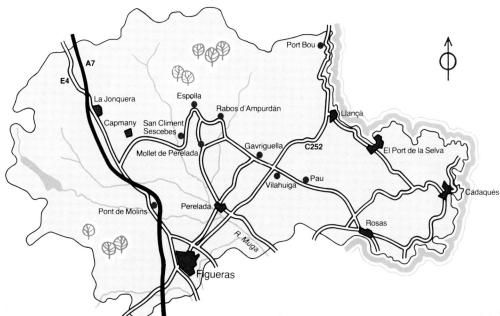

suggest. Every wine town –
Capmany, Mollet, Espolla,
Ricardell, Pont de Molins – has a co-
operative advertising the sale of wine
at the bodega door. Visitors are
usually welcomed.

Touring

This region is also a lovely spot for a
holiday. Although on the crowded
Costa Brava, it is well to the North
of the mass tourist areas. If you are
based on the coast, excursions can be
made to the lovely old town of
Figueras with its Dali museum, or to
the archaeological site of Ampurias.
The wine country is a mere 30-
minute drive away, and a day or two
can be spent visiting the co-
operatives, the quaint Bodegas
Oliveda in Capmany, which
produces a representative range of
wines, or the grander Cavas del
Ampurdán in Perelada.

Perelada

The town of Perelada is dominated
by its mediaeval complex which

dates back to the 14th century and
consists of the Carmen de Perelada
church with its charming Gothic
cloister, and the Castle-Palace with
its two crenellated towers. Under the
church is a system of cellars where
wine has been made since the
church's foundation, and which now
houses an interesting wine museum
as well as being used to age the
firm's premium CAVA brand, Gran
Claustro.

Both the wine company and the
historic buildings are owned by the
same family, who have added a
casino, occupying some of the halls
of the old castle.

Going south

From the Ampurdán, the wine route
leads south to the Denomination of
Alella. As explained on page 100, you
can either take the coast road or the
A7, leaving it at the exit for
Granollers. Both roads should be
avoided on Sunday nights, when they
are busy with Barcelonans on their
way home from the weekend.

CAPMANY
Oliveda S.A. Clle La Roca
3, Capmany. Tel: 54 90 12
(Carles Freixa). Tues-Fri
0900–1300, 1500–1900.
TF. WS. T. Unique
collection of barrel taps.

**FIGUERAS AND
CADAQUES
Recommended
restaurants:**
Restaurante Ampurdán
Ctra N11 Km 763.
(attached to the hotel, just
outside Figueras). Tel: 50 05
62. '*Haute cuisine*' with a
Catalan flavour.

Alternatively, try any of
the restaurants along the
waterfront of the small
town of Cadaqués.

**PERELADA
Recommended museum:**
**Castillo de Pereleda
Museum** Pl. del Carmen,
Perelada. Every day except
Sun p.m., tours: 1000, 1100,
1200, 1630, 1730, 1830.
Exceptional glass and
ceramics collection, wine
museum, library.

Behind the arcades of the late mediaeval cloister of Carmen de Perelada church lies a number of exhibition halls where the greatest collection of glass and ceramics in the country is displayed. There is also a celebrated library with over 6,000 volumes.

ALELLA
Alella Vinícola Soc. Co-op. Rambla Angel Guimera 70, 08328 Alella. Tel: 55 50 842 (Sñrta Asumción Luca). Mon-Fri 0900–1300, 1500–1800. Closed July and Aug. TF. WS. E. Modernist architecture.

Recommended wine shop:
El Xarel.lo Angel Guimera 42, Alella. Wide selection all regions of Spain.

Alella

Only a 40-minute drive from the centre of Barcelona, Alella is a Denomination that has all but vanished. It is already in the stranglehold of the city's creeping industrial estates, and its pleasant countryside has made it a prey for property developers. Today, with its 400 hectares of vines, it is one of the smallest delimited wine areas in the world.

Its survival, however, now appears secure, for the grape-growers, mostly grouped into a co-operative, have stopped the granting of construction licences on delimited land, and any developments that now occur are carefully controlled.

The bodegas

A visit to the region should not take more than a day. Alella Vinícola, the region's co-operative, stands on the main road. The building's facade dates back to its foundation in 1906 but behind is a winery that belongs to the 1980s. The old oak vats and barrels have largely been ripped out and replaced with shiny stainless steel fermentation tanks, with ceramic floors and walls. It may not be as picturesque as in the past, but it is certainly efficient. And this is the only company in the region that still makes the old oak-aged wines.

Parxet, the region's other firm, has two wineries: one in Viana which produces CAVA; the second in Santa María de Martorelles on the western side of the Maresme hills, which produces still wines. Of the two, the second is the more interesting, purpose-built in 1981 but attached to an old *casa de payes* or farm. This was built in the 18th century and has an original wine-making room maintained like a tiny museum.

Barcelona

Situated between the Denominations of Alella and the Penedès, Barcelona sits squarely on the path of the north-south route. To bypass it is simple enough: it is encircled by a complete system of *autopistas*, the busiest in Spain. From the North the driver has only to follow the signs to Tarragona and Lérida (and Gerona and France from the other direction) and the city can be left behind within an hour.

The city itself is well worth a visit. Since it was awarded the 1992 Olympics, it has come under the international spotlight and Europe has realized what the Spanish knew all along – that Barcelona is one of its greatest cities.

Much is written about its cultural life. Catalonia has an artistic tradition as independent as its political tradition. It has many museums, including one of Catalonian art, and much splendid architecture. What is most striking, however, is the sheer style and vitality of Barcelona's people.

This is one of Spain's most prosperous cities, and the combination of wealth and sophistication has created a vibrant gastronomic culture. Marimar Torres in her book *The Spanish Table* estimates that the city has up to 10,000 eating establishments. Its restaurants range from the most sophisticated and expensive in the country to interesting and good value *tapas* bars, where you can drink and enjoy the variety of small tasty dishes.

Like all major cities, however, it has its problems. Traffic congestion is acute, particularly during the rush hour on Sunday nights, and parking is difficult. A word of warning: do not leave anything of value in your car, and carry your cameras and handbags discreetly.

BARCELONA
Recommended wine shops:
Try the wine departments of the two **Corte Inglés** department stores.

A good alternative is **Vinos Lafuente** Clle Juan Sebastian Bach, Barcelona.

Recommended restaurant:
Los Caracoles Clle Escudillers, Barcelona. Traditional Catalan. (Be warned: in this part of Barcelona, near the *ramblas*, be careful of jewellery, wallets and handbags.)

Covered market:
For those interested in food, the Boqueria food market is one of the best in Spain, with exceptional ranges of fish, meat, vegetables, etc. Open every day except Sun. Near the Opera House and the *ramblas*.

The ramblas *(pedestrian parade) in the centre of Barcelona tend to be packed with locals and tourists, both in daytime and at night – an evening tour of the bars here can be a memorable experience.*

The Penedès and CAVA

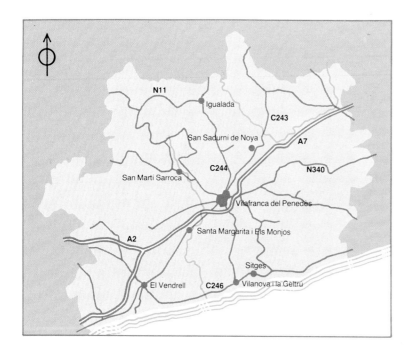

One of Spain's most prestigious wine companies, Bodegas Torres in Vilafranca, has preserved huge old wine presses in the bodega courtyard.

With its bursts of expansion and periods of decline, its peak of prosperity in the 19th century followed by its destruction by the phylloxera, the history of the Penedès is not unlike that of Spain's other Mediterranean wine regions. What sets it apart is its strong recovery in the 20th century. Today it is one of Spain's most prestigious white wine producers as well as being the home of CAVA, one of the great success stories of the Spanish wine industry.

The success of CAVA

The region has undergone great changes since the phylloxera struck. When Josep Raventós opened the first bottle of Spanish sparkling wine in 1872, red wine was still being produced here. Such was the immediate success of CAVA, however, that when the vineyards were replanted, it was mostly with

VILAFRANCA
Bodegas Miguel Torres
Clle Comercio 22, 08720
Vilafranca. Tel: 890 01 00
(Alberto Fornos). Mon-Fri
0900–1200, 1500–1800.
Closed Aug. TF. WS. E. T.
Brandy distillery. (See also
page 108.)

Wine museum
Pl. Jaume I, Vilafranca.
Daily except Sun.
Exceptional collection of
agricultural and wine-
making equipment.

white varieties. Today red wines are produced, some of which have achieved international acclaim, but they represent less than 20 per cent of total production.

'Designer' white wines

CAVA's astonishing success has had other effects on the region. Its appetite for grapes and wine is almost insatiable and many small grape-growers, wine-makers and co-operatives make a comfortable living out of supplying it. The huge profits it has generated, therefore, have percolated their way down through the entire structure and have led to enormous investment in the region's production base, which is now the most advanced in Spain.

The Penedès producers have other advantages. The climate is consistent, enabling them to produce wines whose quality varies little from year to year. In the Parellada, the Macabeo and the Xarel.lo, they have good native grape varieties that blend perfectly together, while the increase in plantings of imported varieties, such as the Chardonnay, will undoubtedly help to add touches of finesse and elegance to the final blended wines.

The result is that the region produces white table wines that are almost tailor-made for the modern palate: pale, light in alcohol (usually 11 to 12 per cent), fruity and with a refreshing cutting edge of acidity.

Vilafranca del Penedès

While San Sadurní is the CAVA capital of Spain, Vilafranca del Penedès, about 40km (25 miles) from central Barcelona on the Tarragona road and with an exit on the A7, is the centre of still-wine production.

The Wine Museum in the centre of Vilafranca del Penedès has the best display of wine-related artefacts in Spain. The collection includes old barrels and manual wine presses.

It is a bustling commercial town that oozes prosperity; there is a wine museum, the only reasonable hotel in the wine country (although travellers may prefer to stay at the more vibrant resort of Sitges), good wine shops and some excellent restaurants nearby. Unfortunately, it has few bodegas worth visiting.

Wine museum

The wine museum is housed in the palace of the Kings of Aragon, dating back to the 12th century. As well as having an unrivalled display of vini- and viticultural equipment, it has sections on art, archaeology and ceramics, so it is well worth a browse, and it also has a bar stocked with most of the wines made in the region.

VILAFRANCA Recommended wine shops:
El Llar del Vi i del Cava del Penedès Ctra Tarragona 3, Vilafranca. Wide selection from Catalonia.

Del Raïm Clle Sant Bernat 3, Vilafranca. Wide selection from all regions of Spain.

SITGES – VILAFRANCA Recommended restaurant:
La Casa del Conill (or **Celler del Penedès**) Anselm Clave 13, S. Miguel de Olerdola. (On the Sitges-Vilafranca road.) Typical Catalan.

LA BLEDA
Rovellats S.A. La Bleda. Tel: 241 40 01 (Sñra Cardona). Mon-Fri 0900–1300, 1500–1730. Closed Aug 15–30. Romanesque chapel, 15th-century *masía*. TF. WS. E. T.

SANTA MARGARITA I ELS MONJOS
Josep Ferret i Mateu Avda Penedès 27, 08730 Santa Margarita i Els Monjos. Tel: 898 01 05 (Joe Quaid). Mon-Fri 0900–1330, 1530–1930 (and Sat a.m.). Closed Aug 1–8. TF. WS. E. T. Underground bottle cellars.

SANT MARTI SARROCA
Celler Hisenda Miret José Anselmo Clavé 7, 08731 Sant Martí Sarroca. Tel: 899 13 56/899 10 28 (Ramón Balada). Mon-Fri 0900–1300, 1500–1830; Sat/Sun 0900–1300. Closed Aug 15–31 and Dec 24–Jan 5. TF. WS. E. T. Compact, high-technology winery.

VILAFRANCA – SANT MARTI
Josep Masachs S.A. Ctra Vilafranca-Sant Martí. Tel: 890 05 93 (Josep Aguado). Mon-Fri 0900–1300, 1500–1900. Closed Aug. TF. WS. E. T. High-technology winery.

Bodegas Torres
The leading still-wine producer of the region is the internationally famous Bodegas Torres, whose old bodega on the Calle del Comercio near the railway station can still be visited. Under the direction of Miguel Torres Jnr, a very famous winemaker, this firm has become one of Spain's greatest flagships, a leading exponent of the judicious use of imported grape varieties and modern production technology. A visit, therefore, is worthwhile if only to taste the wines.

Other still-wine producers
The other noteworthy bodegas that specialize in still wines are all outside the town. The ramshackle winery of Ferret and Mateu, built over a honeycomb of small cellars, is on the N340 in Santa Margarita i Els Monjos and makes good young wines. Very different in style (and, unfortunately, closed to the public) is Jean León in Torrelavid: owned by a Catalan restaurateur in Beverly Hills, it makes outstanding Cabernet Sauvignons and Chardonnays, not unlike those of California. Celler Hisenda Miret in Sant Marti Sarroca makes worthy varietals (wines made from single grape varieties), from the

three classic varieties of the region in a tiny winery that is all stainless steel and shiny tiles.

This last visit has an added bonus. Sant Marti has a lovely Romanesque church and, from the square in front, there is an incomparable view across the rolling terrain of the Penedès, with its vineyards and wineries, to the jagged outline of Montserrat.

Into the CAVA country
From Vilafranca and the still-wine producers, drive to San Sadurni, capital of the mighty CAVA industry. The town is some 10km (8 miles) from Vilafranca along the C243 which winds its way through the vineyards. To appreciate the size of the CAVA industry, however, you should do this trip at the height of the *vendimia*. What is usually a pleasant 15-minute drive becomes an astonishing experience as you mix with the long procession of tractors hauling grapes to the crushers of the giant firms. It then becomes easy to appreciate that Spain is one of the largest exporters of *méthode champenoise* sparkling wines in the world, with an annual production of about 120 million bottles.

The CAVA producers enjoy all the advantages of their still-wine making colleagues. They have the same consistent weather, the same advanced production base and the same native grape varieties with a sprinkling of imported ones.

This last point is particularly important to the industry, for most sparkling wine regions of the world have adopted the grapes used in Champagne. CAVA's allegiance to its own varieties enables it to produce wines with a distinctive character. In general they can be described as warmer than those made in the North, earthier, with less acidity and with excellent body and flavour.

CAVA

With its production regulated by a Consejo Regulador, CAVA is the Denomination for Spanish sparkling wines produced by the *méthode champenoise*. The most important elements to this process are that the wines must undergo their second fermentation in the bottle in which they will be sold (as opposed to the Denomination GRANVAS where the second fermentation takes place in airtight vats), and they must be aged for a minimum of nine months before being released for sale.

During these nine months, the bottles go through a process known as *removido* where, starting from a horizontal position, they are slowly turned until they are upside down with the sediment lying on the cork. This is done either by hand or in large racks known as *girasoles*. They are then disgorged in a dramatic process called *deguelle* when they are uncorked and the sediment removed, topped up with *licor de tiraje*, a mixture of still wine and sugar syrup, and recorked.

The amount of sugar syrup added determines the level of sweetness and the style of the wine. **Brut de Brut** has no sugar syrup added. **Brut Nature** or **Nature** has a very low dosage of sugar or none at all. **Brut** or **Dry** has 2 to 4 grams of sugar per litre. **Seco** or **Extra Dry** has 15 to 17 grams per litre. **Semi-seco** or **Semi-dry** has 22 to 24 grams per litre. **Semi-dulce** or **Semi-sweet** has 33 to 35 grams per litre. And **Dulce** or **Sweet** has over 50 grams per litre.

Codorníu's winery at San Sadurní de Noya (see page 110) is a superb example of Catalonian Modernist architecture, with characteristic neo-Gothic ornament.

SAN SADURNI DE NOYA

Codorníu S.A. San Sadurní de Noya. Tel: 891 01 25 (Sñr Marti). Mon-Fri 0800–1300, 1500–1900. Closed Jul 30–Aug 15. TF. WS. E. T. National monument with wine museum, cellars

Freixenet S.A. Joan Sala 2, San Sadurní de Noya. Tel: 891 07 00 (Sñr Argany). Mon-Fri 0900–1200, 1500–1800. Closed Aug. TF. WS. E. T. (Ask here about **Segura Viudas S.A.**, an associated company housed in a 12th-century *masía*.)

Antonio Mestres Sagües Pl. Ayuntamiento 8, San Sadurní de Noya. Tel: 891 00 43 (Sñrta Luisa). Mon-Fri 0900–1300, 1500–1900. Closed Aug. TF. WS. T.

MONISTROL DE NOYA
**Marqués de Monistrol
S.A.** Monistrol de Noya.
Tel: 593 24 00 (Luis
Agustí). Mon-Fri 0900–
1300, 1400–1800. Closed
July 15–Aug 15. TF. E. T.

*At Marqués de Monistrol the
removido process (see page
109) is still done manually (the
bottles are gradually tilted until
they are upside down).*

San Sadurni de Noya

San Sadurni de Noya is not the most
exciting or beautiful of towns, but it
has several important wineries, the
first of which is the giant Codorníu
on the outskirts of the town. Built by
José Maria Puig i Cadafalch at the
end of the last century, it is a leading
example of modernist industrial
architecture and is now a national
monument. It rises amid beautifully
laid-out gardens and beneath it are
five storeys of cellars, extending for
a total of 26km (16 miles), which
visitors are led through on miniature
trains. The winery also has an
impressive wine museum.

Its arch rival, Freixenet, is on the
other side of town close to the
railway station, and stands out
because of its yellow and white
exterior. It is not as imposing as
Codorníu but again is one of the
giants of the region, producing a
comprehensive range of wines.

These two wineries dominate the
town, but there are others that are
worth a visit. Segura Viudas, close to
the town, is also owned by Freixenet.
Mestres is a family-owned firm on the
main square, where the family has
lived for over 500 years. And there is
the larger, very prestigious Juve y
Camps on the road that leads down
to Freixenet, one of the most modern
wineries of them all, but closed to
visitors.

The country bodegas

Out in the surrounding countryside
there are plenty of other firms to
visit. Marqués de Monistrol, for
example, founded in 1882 and now
a subsidiary of Martini, is housed in
beautiful old buildings in the small
hamlet of Monistrol, surrounded by
its vineyards. Masachs has a brand
new winery just off the Vilafranca-
Sant Martí Sarroca road. Rovellats
has a wonderful old *masía* or country
house dating back to the 15th
century in La Bleda nearby. These
firms represent the small to medium-
sized end of the sector and offer a
pleasing contrast to the two giants
of San Sadurní. And there are many
more small firms dotted around the
region.

Further travel

From the Penedès the traveller has
two choices: either to follow the
N340 or the A7 to Tarragona, or to
take an excursion to the Raimat
estate, near Lérida.

The Raimat Estate

When Manuel Raventós, the owner of Codorníu, bought the Raimat estate, it was described as '3,000 hectares with a castle and one tree'. There was no rainfall and the land was a desert. Today Raimat is transformed and, after years of struggle, produces what are considered among the best table wines and CAVAS in Catalonia, made from a mixture of grapes. This visit can be combined with one to the mediaeval monastery of Poblet (off the A2).

Water came with a new canal, and Raventós brought in new soil, flattening nearby hills and spreading the earth on his vast hectarage. When the soil proved to have too high a salt content, fruit trees were planted to leach it out. This has now been declared a 'model agricultural estate' by the Spanish Government.

It has its own railway station and a workers' village; and cereals and fruit trees are planted, along with 1,000 hectares of vines, most of them of imported grape varieties.

The estate's winery has buildings of 1918 and a second part, completed in 1988, built in the shape of a pyramid, with its slopes covered in grass and a vineyard on top. It is well worth a visit.

The route

From Vilafranca del Penedès take either the A7 and A2 to Lérida or drive to Igualada and join the N11. In Lérida follow the signs for Huesca and the N240, and the estate is some 15km (9 miles) outside the city.

The estate is open to serious visitors on working days, but you should make an appointment first by telephoning Codorníu in Barcelona.

The vines at Raimat are trained on wires and regimented with maximum efficiency.

Tarragona

By comparison with Barcelona,
Tarragona is a quiet provincial city.
with good hotels and restaurants, a
fine *rambla* (parade) that leads up to
a *mirador* or viewpoint over the sea,
and a lovely mediaeval quarter. If
you are looking for evidence of the
grandeur of Spain's Roman past,
this is the place to go.

Up until recently this was also a
wine city. In the 18th century, great
wine trading houses established their
offices near the port, as they did in
Valencia, buying wine from
producers and co-operatives in the
interior, improving and exporting it.
Today most of these firms have fled
the confines of the city and have
moved to more modern sites on the
outskirts. Only one remains, De
Muller, originally founded by a
German in 1851. Its old oak vats and
lovely interior courtyard give an
insight into the city's past and, as the
company produces a fascinating

*The Puente del Diablo, or Devil's Bridge, lies
to the north of Tarragona, just off the
motorway. This Roman aqueduct is one of
Tarragona's great historic legacies.*

range of fortified wines, it is worth a
visit. The company has also made a
name for itself as a producer of altar
wines, and has supplied the Vatican
since the turn of the century.

Lopez Bertrán
The space-age winery of Lopez
Bertrán is a complete contrast to De
Muller. It is on the N240, a short
drive from the city. Where De
Muller is all oak and old buildings,
Bertrán is stainless steel tanks and
advanced bottling lines. To spend a
day visiting these two bodegas is to
see the two extremes of the Spanish
industry today and, in between
visits, an excellent lunch may be had
at the C'al Brut in the Serallo district
of Tarragona, one of the best fish
restaurants in Spain.

The Mountains of Catalonia

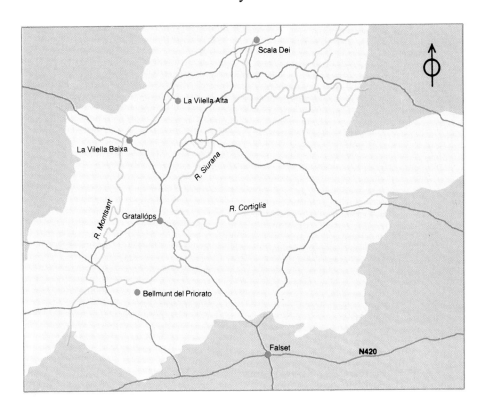

The hairpin bends and steep gradients of the wine country of the interior make driving very difficult, and if you have a caravan it is advisable to leave it behind when venturing inland. But motoring problems aside, a day or two in this area can be really memorable.

From Tarragona, your route takes you along the N420 to the prosperous agricultural city of Reus, and then continues to Falset. A short way from Reus the road climbs, giving some spectacular views before reaching a high pass, and then descending to the town.

In Falset you are still in the Denomination of Tarragona, but the wines are very different. For while most of its wines are white, this area produces strong full-bodied reds, mostly in the town's co-operative, founded in 1919.

The Priorato

Travelling on to the Priorato, you venture into very different country. The sheer beauty of the wild, rugged terrain with its jagged peaks and stone outcrops; the shine of its soils of decomposed slate; its decaying villages built up the mountain slopes and its abandoned lead mines that date back to Roman times make this one of the most fascinating corners of Spain.

Unfortunately, this is a region that is dying fast. Its climate and soil produce some of the best olive oil, figs and hazelnuts in Spain, and some of its most unique wines. But the low yield of its fruit trees and vines, often planted on almost inaccessible slopes and terraces, make it difficult to earn a living from the land. The young people have long since departed.

BELLMUNT DEL PRIORATO
Masia Barril Bellmunt del Priorato. Tel: 830 1 92. Visiting days and hours are flexible, but must be arranged in advance. TF. WS. T. Picnic area, medicinal herb garden.

GRATALLOPS
Celler Cecilio August Vicent i Robert, Gratallóps. Tel: 83 91 81. Open during business hours. No appointment needed. TF (from the barrel). WS (they will fill up any container you provide). Old barrels and implements.

SCALA DEI
Cellers Scala Dei S.A. Rambla de la Cartoixa, 43379 Scala Dei. Tel: 82 70 27 (Sñr Peyra). Daily 1100–1300, 1600–1900. TP. WS. T. Ask here for permission to visit the ruined abbey.

The wineries
The first stop is the small, family-owned winery of Masia Barril in Bellmunt. After the modern bodegas of the North, Barril will come as a surprise. The owner transports the grapes from his vineyards by mule, crushes them in a tiny, antique crusher and bottles them by hand. These are the traditional wines of the region, almost black in colour, packed with fruit, extract and tannin, and very alcoholic (sometimes up to 15 per cent).

From Bellmunt you proceed to Gratallóps for a quick visit to Bodegas Cecilio. Housed in a building that is over 250 years old, this winery consists of no more than one large room with barrels stacked against the walls and a collection of old bottles and flasks. The owners, however, will cheerfully pour you samples of dark, intensely perfumed and fruity wine from the barrel as long as you are prepared to buy a bottle for a few pesetas. You may like to stop for lunch at the rustic Racó del Priorato restaurant in La Vilella Baixa, a typical village of the area, before the day's tour reaches its climax at Scala Dei.

Scala Dei
Lying below the Sierra de Montsant, Scala Dei is a hamlet that served the first Carthusian monastery to be built in Spain in 1162. The tiny central square is flanked by large, solid houses belonging to the four families that form the Scala Dei Association. This group owns the town's winery, built originally by the monks. Today, however, it is well equipped with modern crushers, stainless steel fermentation tanks and oak barrels for ageing, and it produces the most sophisticated wines of the region – from young reds, whites and rosés, to red oak-aged *reservas*. Just up the road, with the Sierra de Montsant in the background, are the ruins of the old monastery, which have been acquired by the Catalan government. The ruins are now preserved, and the grounds will be converted into gardens.

Terra Alta
The last Denomination of the interior is Terra Alta, which can be reached by following the N420 and then the N230 from Falset to Gandesa.

Terra Alta means the 'high land': it is on a high plateau 400m (1,300 ft) above sea level. The region produces mostly white wines which are famed for their intensity and aroma, as well as full-bodied, strapping reds and interesting *rancios*. Again, the table wines are high in alcohol, although there are some firms, with an eye on the modern consumer, that have managed to lighten them to about 12.5 per cent.

There are two privately-owned firms in Gandesa that are worth visiting; the modern Pedro Rovira, which also has a bodega in the Tarragona D.O., and Bodegas J. Pedrola: both make 'modern' light wines. Otherwise the co-operative on the Avenida de Cataluña makes wines in the more traditional style.

Further travel
From Gandesa the N230 leads down to the ancient city of Tortosa and the coastal A7 and N340 to Valencia. Otherwise, from the Priorato, you have to retrace your steps to Reus which is a few kilometres from the same road just to the South of the city of Tarragona.

Deep in the interior of the Priorato the old abbey of Scala Dei now lies in picturesque ruins, with the Sierra de Montsant forming an imposing rocky backdrop. The Catalan government has declared the abbey a Garden Monument.

LA VILELLA BAIXA
Recommended restaurant:
Racó del Priorato La Vilella Baixa. Tel: 83 90 65. Rural Catalan cuisine.

115

Food and Festivals

FOOD SPECIALITIES

Arroz Negre Literally 'black rice': one of Catalonia's answers to paella. Rice cooked in a large, two-handled frying pan with shellfish, particularly squid, which gives the dish its colour.

Escudella i Carn d'Olla A very traditional, rustic Catalan dish which is a favourite at Christmas. A veal or beef stew with vegetables, *butifarra* sausage served whole and a *pilota*, a long roll of minced beef and pork flavoured with garlic, cinnamon and pine nuts. The broth is made into a pasta soup and served as an entrée.

Habas a la Catalana Broad beans stewed in white wine with black *butifarra*, and thick slices of bacon and onions.

Parrillada Fish, shellfish or meat simply grilled over an open fire and served with a variety of different sauces.

Pato con Higos A very typical dish of the Ampurdán, duck roasted in a little brandy or sherry with figs, dried or fresh.

Zarzuela One of the classic dishes of Catalonia, a fish casserole which can be extremely elaborate. Some chefs use only shellfish such as clams, mussels, prawns and lobster. Others mix in chunks of fish such as hake.

Other stews to look out for are the *Suquet* or *Romesco de Pescados*.

CATALONIAN CUISINE

Catalonia is generally considered to have the most varied and sophisticated cuisine in Spain. As is the case in most of the country's northerly regions, its chefs have a wide variety of excellent local ingredients at their disposal, but what sets them apart is the flair and imagination of combinations such as *Pato con Higos*, duck with figs; *Codornices con Pasas y Piñones*, quail with raisins and pine nuts; and *Conejo con Peras y Nabos*, rabbit with pears and turnips.

Fresh ingredients
The coast, of course, produces good fish which is either served in a stew, such as the *Zarzuela*, or grilled with sauces in the excellent *Parrilladas*. In addition the fertile Ebro valley to the South of Tarragona is the source of wonderful rice (combined with squid in *Arroz Negre)*, fruit and vegetables. Further inland the more wooded areas yield an abundance of small game, herbs, mushrooms, particularly the unique *rovellons*, and the very popular pine nuts. Veal, chicken, goose and pork are all used, the last being the basis of the typical *butifarra* sausages, with pine nuts, cinnamon, almonds and cumin.

Catalan sauces
It is sauces, however, that are the great Catalan speciality. There is the famous *allioli*, made with garlic and olive oil; the *romesco* of Tarragona, which can be very hot, made with garlic, small peppers, tomatoes, bread and roasted almonds; *samfaina*, with sautéed onions, aubergines, courgettes and tomatoes; and *picada*, with saffron, garlic, hazelnuts, almonds, parsley and cinnamon. These sauces are served either to accompany grilled shellfish, fish or

meat, or form the basis of a Catalan stew such as the famous *Romesco de Pescados*.

FESTIVALS

Vilafranca del Penedès celebrates its wine festival every odd-numbered year (1989, 1991 etc) in April or May, when wine stands are set up in the town's central square. Otherwise, most of the region's wine festivals are in early September: the Feria del Vino in Figueras, which takes place in the first week of September; or the Fiesta de la Varema when the harvest's first must is blessed in the central square of Alella. Perhaps the most original, from a gastronomic point of view, is San Majín in Tarragona in August which includes a *romesco* sauce competition in the Serallo district.

The most famous fiesta sight of the region are Tarragona's *Castellers* or *Xiquets de Valls*, pyramids formed by young men dressed in local costumes at the big fiestas of Reus, Valls, El Vendrell and Tarragona, and the Fiesta Mayor of Vilafranca at the end of August. In general, however, the region has nothing as spectacular as San Fermín, the Fallas or the Feria de Abril in Seville.

Participants in the festival at Vilafranca from Castellers *or* Xiquets de Valls, *human castles. These acrobatic displays originated in Tarragona, but they are now traditional in most fiestas of southern Catalonia.*

The Levante and the Islands _____

Embracing five Denominations of Origin – Alicante, Jumilla, Yecla, Utiel-Requena and Valencia – the Levante has vineyards in the provinces of Castellón, Valencia, Alicante and Murcia. A sixth Denomination, Almansa, which is more Levantine than Manchegan in character, is included in this chapter, although it is sometimes grouped with the neighbouring Denominations of Castilla-La Mancha.

The Levante can be divided into two parts: the interior, with the Denominations of Utiel-Requena, Almansa, Yecla and Jumilla; and the coastal stretch which includes the Denominations of Valencia and Alicante. The contrast between the two, the one with its small towns, arid mountains and gorges and the other with its fertile plains covered with orange groves, paddy fields and vineyards, its two great cities and its coastal resorts, could not be greater, and adds excitement to a wine tour of the region. Combined with the excellent climate, the wonderful food and the great variety of wines, it makes travelling in this part of the country especially delightful.

The wine regions of the Levante can be visited following two routes. You can make your base in Valencia and Alicante, and then make one or two-day excursions into the interior (from Valencia into the Denominations of Valencia and Utiel-Requena; from Alicante into Alicante, Jumilla, Yecla and Almansa). Or, and this is the suggested route, start in Valencia and then make a circular sweep through the wine regions, ending up in Alicante. The advantages of this latter route are that you avoid the crowded coast (which has some of the most commercialized and degraded seaside resorts in Spain), and that you travel through some spectacular countryside, particularly between Requena and Almansa.

Valencia is about 270km (168 miles) from Tarragona (where the tour of Catalonia ended), along the A7 or the N332, both of which follow

the coast. After spending a few days in Valencia you can take the N111 in the direction of Madrid to Chiva and then up to the edges of the great plateau of La Mancha and the towns of Utiel and Requena.

The Sierras and Southwards
From Requena the difficult N330 leads through some fascinating mountainous terrain and then descends to the wine town of Almansa in the province of Albacete. From here you can either travel to Villena, one of the main wine towns of the Denomination of Alicante, or cross the border into Murcia along the small C3223 to Yecla and then the C3314 to Jumilla. The city of Murcia is then only 120km (75 miles) away, a worthwhile detour. Otherwise, continue to the C3213 to Monóvar, the other important centre in the D.O. Alicante, before joining the N330 to Alicante itself.

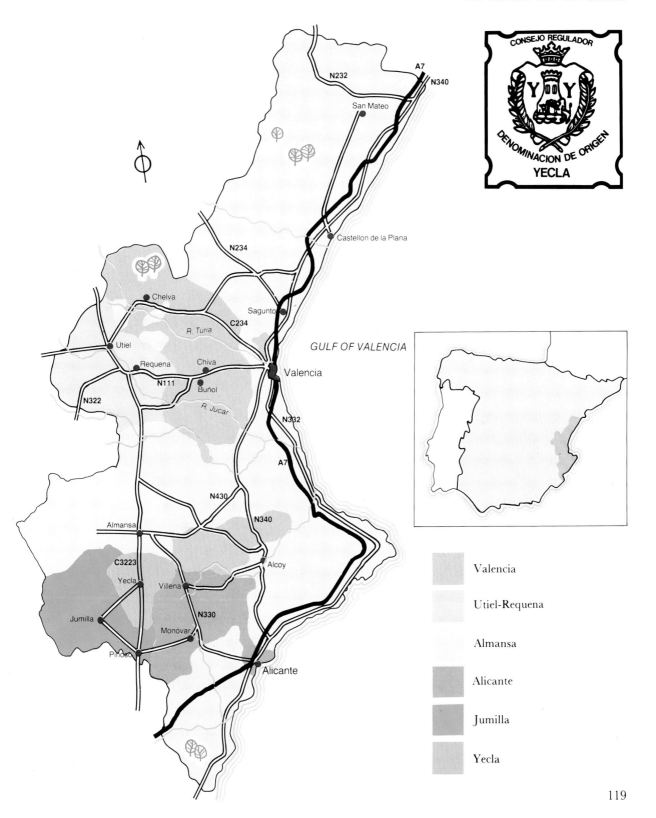

CONSEJO REGULADOR

DENOMINACION DE ORIGEN

YECLA

N232

A7

N340

San Mateo

Castellon de la Plana

N234

Chelva

Sagunto

C234

R. Turia

Utiel

Requena

Chiva

N111

Buñol

N322

R. Jucar

GULF OF VALENCIA

Valencia

N332

A7

N430

N340

Almansa

C3223

Yecla

Villena

Alcoy

Jumilla

N330

Monóvar

Pinoso

Alicante

Valencia

Utiel-Requena

Almansa

Alicante

Jumilla

Yecla

The Wines of the Levante

Grape varieties

The six Denominations of the Levante cover some 164,000 hectares of vineyard and produce about 3,850,000 hectolitres of wine a year.

The principal grape varieties are the white Merseguera and the red Monastrell. Also authorized and planted in smaller quantities are the red Bobal (the predominant variety of Utiel-Requena), the Garnacha Tintorera and the Cencibel (the Tempranillo), and the white Macabeo and Planta Nova which is indigenous to the region. There are also some small plantings of imported varieties but these are still on an experimental basis.

The wine industry of the Levante first flourished when the Romans established themselves around the city of Sagunto at the end of the second Punic War. Periods of expansion and retraction, particularly during the Moorish occupation, have followed. But in general, the wine industry has thrived since the Christian Reconquest.

By the 18th century wine merchants from Bordeaux were strengthening their wine with the stronger, deeper-coloured wines from Valencia, a trade that reached its climax when France was struck by the phylloxera. This boom, however, was short-lived. The

The vast VINIVAL winery in El Grao has been dubbed 'the cathedral', and is one of the city's best-known landmarks. It is also one of the largest wineries in Spain, with its own railway siding.

French industry recovered, protected by high duties on imported wines, and the phylloxera reached the Levante in 1900.

Replanting

Although the disease did not affect the region as badly as other parts of the country (Jumilla, for example, is largely phylloxera-free), it led to a great geographical restructuring: when the vineyards on the littoral plains were destroyed, their rich alluvial soil was replanted with citrus fruit, almonds and garden vegetables. The vines were forced inland to the arid mountains where the soil was too poor to sustain other crops. Coincidentally, they thrived in the cooler climate. Today, Utiel-Requena is one of the few parts of Spain where the area of land under vine is expanding.

The export tradition

The phylloxera, however, did not affect the region's strong exporting tradition. For, although Jumilla and Yecla have created a strong market in the southern part of the country, the other regions have always looked abroad for their sales, a practice that dates back to Roman times when the wines of the Levante were exported all over the Mediterranean. Today the port of Valencia handles some 40 per cent of Spain's total wine exports with the giant VINIVAL alone shipping 100 million litres a year.

Bulk shipments

This is an impressive achievement, but it disguises an important weakness. Some 80 per cent of these exports are in bulk, destined to be blended with the wines of other countries or to be bottled under the brand of a supermarket or retail chain. Profit margins are slim, and although the producers are able to put bottles on foreign shelves at an attractive price, this generates little capital for investment in vineyards and production facilities. For a long time, while other regions such as the Penedès and the Rioja raced ahead, updating their wineries and improving their vineyards, the Levante stood still. It is only recently that the region has begun to invest and to modernize, and it is still some way behind the times.

Variety and quantity

This is still an immensely important wine region, however. It produces more wine than any other part of Spain except La Mancha, and its wines are varied. Recent improvements in production facilities have enabled the big Valencian firms

to make a new generation of good-value everyday drinking wines.

The great red wine areas – Alicante, Jumilla, Yecla and Almansa – continue to produce their traditional red wines, big in body, strong in alcohol and deep in colour. These may not be to everybody's taste, but they could never be described as lacking in character. Utiel-Requena, with its cooler climate, produces some excellent young whites and rosés; while all over the region some fascinating fortified wines are made, culminating in the glorious, copper-coloured, oak-aged Fondillón of Alicante.

Valencia's great cathedral, which stands on the site of an ancient mosque in the centre of the city, has an octagonal Gothic tower called the Miguelete (literally 'Little Michael').

Valencia

Lace and mantillas are part of traditional Levantine costumery. This parade is part of the Fallas of Valencia (see page 131).

**VALENCIA
Recommended
restaurants:**
El Commodoro, Transit 3,
Valencia. Tel: 351 38 15.
Sophisticated and
expensive.
La Dehesa Playa del Soler.
Tel: 323 69 40. On the
beach, just outside the city.
Rice dishes a speciality.

Covered market:
Valencia's covered food
market in the centre is a
must for anyone interested
in food and shopping. Go
early in the morning.

After Madrid and Barcelona,
Valencia is Spain's third city. The
nearby port of El Grao is the largest
in the country, shipping a wide
range of Spanish goods abroad:
clothes, computers, cars, fruit and
vegetables, and, of course, vast
quantities of wine. Until quite
recently, the city and the port were
separate, two cities in their own
right. Today, urban sprawl has
linked them together.

Valencia does not have the
archaeological interest of Tarragona,
the unique architecture of the great
southern cities, or the culture and
vitality of Barcelona or Madrid. But
it has a wonderfully relaxed
atmosphere, a constant ebb and flow
of sun-tanned people walking the

tree-lined avenues in the evening or
sitting in the outdoor restaurants
and bars. The inhabitants enjoy their
sunny climate and also bask in the
wealth of this industrial and fertile
area. Once a year, the natural
exuberance of the people finds
expression in the colourful festival of
Fallas (see also page 131).

The city's wine trade
Valencia is not really a 'wine city'.
In its bars, the favourite drinks are
beer and cocktails and, if wine is
ordered, it is more likely to be a
Rioja or a Penedès. In fact, Valencia
exports more wine than any other
Spanish city, but its wine companies
are export businesses, which have
traditionally paid little attention to

the home market. The trade is dominated by five enormous firms, three of which are Swiss-owned. And although two of them have some vineyards, they are brokers rather than producers by tradition, buying wine from the co-operatives and the small firms of the interior, filtering and blending it to the clients' specifications and shipping it from the port.

Levantine investments

These companies represent the dynamic, progressive sector of the Levante's wine industry. They are well aware that there is a great international demand for light, well-made table wine, and in recent years they have invested heavily in their wineries, with new stainless steel storage and fermentation tanks, better filtering and laboratory equipment, and new, super-efficient bottling lines. They can now produce cleaner, fresher and fruitier light wines than previously.

The 'wine bazaar'

The result of all this exporting of wine is that Valencia is now the greatest 'wine bazaar' in Spain. An extraordinary array of goods is prepared for shipment in the wineries: great black demijohns of strong red wine for West Africa; rustic-looking wicker-covered flasks for Germany; blue barrels of wine concentrate for Japan; and pallets of canned Sangria (a spiced and sweetened wine drink) for the United States. It is an extraordinary sight, not an appealing one for the wine connoisseurs, and it almost disguises the fact that these firms now produce some of the best value everyday drinking wine in Spain.

The great wine companies

The largest of these companies is the giant VINIVAL in El Grao. Its extraordinary modern winery, nicknamed the 'cathedral' by some, and less flattering names by others, can be seen from the A7 as one approaches the city. Its brown brick exterior looks like a collection of upturned cigar tubes (see page 120).

Inside, however, the equipment is all modern, while in a separate building, two fast bottling lines are constantly in action, demonstrating just what extraordinary quantities of wine are involved in this modernized industry.

Also in El Grao are the three Swiss-owned firms: Bodegas Schenk, Augusto Egli and Cherubino Valsangiacomo. All three are housed in their original buildings, but while Cherubino Valsangiacomo still has its old oak vats and barrels, in the other two these have now mostly been replaced. All three produce a wide range of wines, and are a hive of activity, as befits some of the largest wine companies in Spain.

Vicente Gandia Pla's brand new winery in Chiva, outside Valencia, is amongst the most advanced in the country (see page 124). This construction would be quite at home in the Napa Valley of California.

VINIVAL S.A. Av. Blasco Ibañez 44, Alboraya, Valencia. Tel: 371 01 11 (Christopher Garrigos). Mon-Fri 0900–1330, 1600–1830. Closed Aug. TF. WS. E. T. Large scale, high-technology winery.

From Valencia to Utiel-Requena

BUNOL
Recommended restaurant:
Venta l'homme Ctra Valencia-Madrid Km 45, Buñol. Tel: 250 18 15. Typically Levantine food.

As there is little room for expansion in El Grao, the last great wine firm of Valencia, Vicente Gandia Pla, has recently moved to the town of Chiva, the first stop of your tour of the Levante interior.

From Valencia, take the busy N111 which leads through orange groves before starting the slow climb to the central plateau of Spain. Here you are deep in the D.O. Valencia, a confusing region with a myriad of microclimates and grape varieties. Although some reds and rosés are made here, this is primarily white wine country with its production based on the Merseguera, not the best variety in Spain but capable of producing very reasonable wines when well vinified: light, fresh and with an adequate level of acidity.

Gandia Pla produces good examples of these and above-average reds and rosés in its brand new, purpose-built winery just off the main road.

Then it is on up the N111 to the 'Venta l'homme' which sits on a bend of the road near the small town of Buñol. This is an old coach house dating back to the 18th century; its regional cuisine makes it an ideal place to stop at lunchtime.

Utiel-Requena

Buñol is also close to the border between the Denomination of Valencia and that of Utiel-Requena, a border marked by the deep furrow of the Cabriel river. As most of the wine from both Denominations is marketed by the big firms of Valencia, the link between them is strong. Furthermore, their wines are complementary: while most of Valencia's production is of white, that of Utiel-Requena is of red and rosé. The region is dominated by the Bobal, a variety that produces acceptable young reds, and rosés that are often regarded as being among the best in the country. Its principal weakness, however, is that its wines do not age well. The local Consejo, therefore, is actively encouraging the planting of varieties with greater staying power so the hectarage of the Cencibel in particular is on the increase.

The co-operatives

The region's production is dominated by the co-operatives, the most typical being those of the towns of Utiel and Requena themselves. A visit to either of these may not be the most interesting on the route, but they are large companies and offer a contrast to the great companies of Valencia.

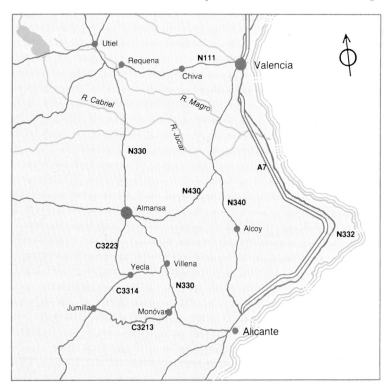

Requena to Almansa

Lying at an altitude of 800m (2,600 ft), Utiel-Requena is close to the borders of both La Mancha and Aragon. This proximity to the old kingdom of the North becomes apparent as you drive from Requena to Almansa along the small N330 that leads through a landscape of fir trees and orchards. Slowly the ochre soil that is so dominant as far south as the province of Teruel begins to blend with the pale yellow of the southern Levante. Then the road plunges down into the valley formed by the Embalse de Embarcaderos. This is a place of great natural beauty with the walls of the valley revealing intermingled layers of ochre and yellow rock and earth. Suddenly two enormous smoke stacks come into view. If you have ever felt anger at man's mutilation of natural beauty, it will well up in you now. For it is this beautiful valley that has been chosen as the site of one of Spain's largest nuclear power stations, complete with a dam and a multiplicity of access roads.

Almansa

Almansa is at the extreme eastern end of the province of Albacete, where La Mancha meets the Levante. Its 'Moors and Christians' festival at the beginning of May is very Levantine in character.

ALMANSA
Bodegas Piqueras Juan Ramón Jimenez 3, Almansa. Tel: 34 14 82 (Mario or Juan Pablo Bonete). Mon-Fri 0800–1300, 1600–1830. TF. WS. T.

Recommended restaurant:
Restaurante Almansa
Ctra Madrid-Valencia Km 340, Almansa. Tel: 734 10 15. Typically Levantine-Manchegan cuisine.

Almansa's mediaeval fortress, perched on its rocky mound, is a local landmark.

Almansa's wines

The region's wines reflect this Levantine allegiance: Almansa is predominantly a red wine-producing region, where the Monastrell rather than the Cencibel rules, and what little white is produced is made from the Merseguera grape rather than the Airén. This is a small Denomination and most of its wine is sold in bulk for blending, and of its two significant producers only one, Bodegas Piqueras, produces wine in bottle (the other is Alfonso Abellán). Housed in a picturesque family-owned winery that was built at the turn of the century, and whose underground bottle deposits have been converted into barrel cellars, this company is well worth a visit. It produces some light whites and rosés and full-bodied reds which have a high but not excessive level of alcohol. Its *reservas*, aged for a minimum of two years in barrel, are also worth tasting.

Alicante's old harbour is guarded by a crag that rises from the sea like the rock of Gibraltar. It lies to the south of the Levante wine route.

Villena and Yecla

From Almansa, the traveller has a choice of two routes: either to go straight to Yecla, or to take a short detour to Villena, some 30km (19 miles) away along the N330.

Villena is a mediaeval city, as its castle testifies, and was once the centre of a strong feudal kingdon which also included Almansa. Today this is one of the two main towns of the D.O. Alicante, and it is the home of the family-run company of García Póveda. Their excellent wine is on sale at the bodega door, but the winery itself is not open to visitors.

Yecla

The road forward goes across the hot, dusty plain – either along the C3314 from Villena, or the C3223 from Almansa – to Yecla, in the next Denomination. The centre of the town itself, with its swirling dust and continuous flow of noisy lorries, is best avoided. But fortunately, the three leading wine companies are on the outskirts of the town: there is the giant but commercially backward co-operative of La Purísima, which is one of the largest in Spain; the more advanced privately-owned Bodegas Castaño; and Enrique Ochoa Palao.

In general the wines that these firms produce are similar to those of Alicante and Jumilla. Little white wine is made and production is based on the Monastrell. The rosés, or *claretes*, are at their best while young and can be reasonably fresh and crisp with a good level of fruit. The muscle-bound reds, however, have more character, if not too much altogether: bulging with extract, fruit and tannin, they have a deep purple, almost black colour when young. The *reservas* are only slightly more approachable, smoother, with less mouth-puckering tannin, brown edges around the rim and sometimes a touch of oxidization on the nose.

These wines are incredibly high in alcohol, sometimes up to 17 or 18 per cent, and even the most advanced companies have not been able to lower the level below about 13 per cent. In the wiltingly hot summers, therefore, the wines can have a dangerous effect.

YECLA
Bodegas Castaño S.A.
Ctra de Fuentealamo, Yecla. Tel: 879 11 15 (Sñrta Conchi). Mon-Fri 0800–1300, 1500–1900. Closed July 15–Aug 8. TF. WS. T.
Enrique Ochoa Palao S.L., Paraje los Quinones, Yecla. Tel: 79 20 64 (Sñr Ochoa/Sñr Sabuco). Mon-Fri 0900–1400, 1700–1900. TF. WS. T.

Viña las Gruesas (above) is the leading brand of Bodegas Castaño, one of Yecla's best wine firms. The modern wine-cooling equipment (left) belongs to Bodegas Enrique Ochoa Palao in Yecla.

Jumilla and Monóvar

An ancient wine press stands guard over the entrance to the Wine Museum of Bodegas Asencio Carcelén in Jumilla. Carcelén is one the most traditional wine companies in the Denomination, and welcomes visitors.

JUMILLA
Bodegas Asencio Carcelén N.C.R. Baron del Solar 1 and 3, Jumilla. Tel: 78 04 18 (Sñr Gerente). Mon-Fri 0900–1400, 1700–1900. Closed Aug. TF. WS. T. 19th-century winery, wine museum.

From Yecla it is another 30km (19 miles) to Jumilla, a quieter, leafier and altogether pleasanter town. While Yecla's economy is based principally on its light industry, especially furniture-making, Jumilla is a real wine town. The aridity of the surrounding countryside makes most other crops unviable and, as the phylloxera has never penetrated its sandy soils, viticulture is cheap. The town has several large companies whose sales have prospered in southern Spain, and even the smaller bodegas of the town are proud to advertise their wines on the door.

Two of the great giants of the town glower at each other from either side of the Murcia road: the enormous, modern co-operative of San Isidro, which produces a sound and representative range of wines: and the privately-owned García Carrión, the king of the tetrapack, whose installations are more like a factory than a winery. The third great giant, Señorio del Condestable, owned by one of Spain's largest wine groups, is closer to the centre and is very different. Its winery rivals those of the northern regions in its modernity and its range of wines, from young reds, whites and rosés to oak-aged *reservas*. These are more 'modern' in style, more approachable than those of other firms, lighter in colour and with less alcohol.

From a touristic point of view, however, it is the old, family-owned and run company of Asencio Carcelén that takes the prizes. Its lovely old winery, with its great old oak vats and barrels, can hardly have changed much since the firm's foundation in 1876. It produces some fascinating wines in the traditional style which can be tasted in the centre of a small but interesting wine museum. A visit to this company is a delightful experience.

Monóvar

The final stop on your route is the town of Monóvar back in the D.O. Alicante, which is approached along the C3213 from Jumilla. This is the second of the Denomination's wine towns, with two interesting, family-owned bodegas: Primitivo Quiles and Salvador Póveda. In their attractive and rather ramshackle wineries, both these companies produce some of the best and most typical table wines of the region. And Salvador Póveda, which is open to visitors, is one of the only firms that still produces what used to be a great regional speciality, the oak-aged and fortified Fondillón. The wine's long ageing, during which some 50 per cent is said to evaporate, gives it a light copper colour and an immense smoothness and intensity. Unfortunately, its production is extremely expensive and small quantities only are made today.

The traditional wines of the southern Levante include (top left) Salvador Póveda's Fondillón, named after the famous writer Azorín, a native of Monóvar; and two leading brands of Asencio Carcelén, Con Sello and Sol y Luna, both from Jumilla.

Further travel

For those restricting themselves to a tour of the Levante, the C3213 meets the larger N330 just after Monóvar, and this leads directly to Alicante. After the heat and heavy wines of the interior, this city, with its beaches, its wonderful restaurants and its thriving night life, is the perfect place to recuperate.

Those looking for further exertions are advised to go southwards to Murcia and then take the N340 and the N342 (not the most exciting of drives) to the fabulous city of Granada, a gateway to the great fortified wine regions of Andalusia. From there a circular route takes in Málaga, Jerez (either along the coast road or through Ronda), and Córdoba, with its neighbouring region of Montilla. Then the route outlined in the earlier chapters of this book can be followed in reverse through the two Castilles and Madrid to the Rioja, and Navarra, ending up either at Bilbao or at the French border at the western end of the Pyrenees.

ALICANTE
Recommended restaurants:
Darsena, Club Náutico, Alicante. Tel: 323 69 40. On the quay in the old harbour. Rice dishes a speciality.
Delfín, Esplanada de España 12, Alicante. Tel: 521 49 11. Levantine. Rice and fish dishes a speciality.
Quo Vadis, Pl. Santísima Trinidad Faz 3, Alicante. Tel: 521 66 60. Levantine. Rice and fish dishes.

MONOVAR
Salvador Póveda S.A., Benjamín Palencia 19, Monóvar. Tel: 547 01 80 (Sñrta Maria José). Mon-Fri 0900–1400, 1600–2000. TF. WS. E. T.

MURCIA
Recommended restaurant:
El Rincón de Pepe Clle Apostoles 34, Murcia. Tel: 21 22 48. Typically southern Levantine cuisine.

Food and Festivals

LEVANTINE CUISINE

The most famous dish of the Levante is the paella. Valencia is Spain's greatest rice producer, growing large quantities of the top quality, short-grained variety in the flat, swampy area around Lake Albufera to the South of the city. The irrigation system here was first built by the Moors. Rice has been the staple diet of the coastal area for centuries, and its people have traditionally added to it what they could afford: fish, snails and vegetables to begin with and, in more recent, prosperous years, more expensive ingredients such as chicken, beef and shellfish. Today, there are countless different types of paella, some of which are wonderfully elaborate, most of them including chicken and shellfish, and coloured with golden saffron.

In the inland areas of Almansa, Utiel-Requena, Jumilla and Yecla, the cuisine is very different. Fish and rice disappear from the menu and are replaced by beans, potatoes and small game, cooked in *ollas* or stews and flavoured with mountain herbs such as thyme and rosemary. The best example is the splendid *Gazpacho Manchego* or *Alicantino*, a true shepherd's dish, hearty and filling, good protection against the colder climate of the interior.

FOOD SPECIALITIES

Doradas a la Sal Fish baked encased in coarse sea salt to keep it moist. Many different kinds of fish are used, but the most popular is the *dorada*.
Gazpacho Alicantino or *Manchego* In contrast to the southern cold soup, this is a strong stew. Its ingredients vary but are usually small game such as partridge and rabbit. In some versions a *torta*, a hard biscuit made with flour and water, is broken up into pieces to absorb the juices; in others the stew is poured over it and, after the meal, the underside is spread with honey as a dessert.
Paella The classic version of this dish combines rice with chicken, beef, vegetables (green beans, peppers and tomatoes), shellfish (mussels, prawns) and squid and snails. A fisherman's version is the *Paella de Mariscos* with only shellfish, while an interesting alternative is the *Paella de Caza* with small game and often snails.

FESTIVALS

The Levante has some spectacular fiestas but not directly related to wine. Virtually every wine town in the region, of course, celebrates the coming of the *vendimia*, when the first must is blessed in the central square, but none of these festivities are particularly remarkable or unique. The best known are those of Requena at the end of August/beginning of September, and of Jumilla about a week earlier.

There are, however, two uniquely Levantine festivals in early spring. These festivals will appeal to those who enjoy spectacular shows and historic celebrations, as well as the traveller who likes to drink wine, and have fun during a great occasion.

The first is the Fallas that takes place in the city of Valencia during the week leading up to St Joseph's Day on 19 March. The usual religious processions and ritual bullfights take place, but they culminate in a blazing orgy of bonfires, when life-size wax figures, some of which have taken six months or more to build, are set alight.

The second other great Levantine celebration is the series of 'Moors and Christians' festivals, which take place in many towns. The most famous is that of the small town of Alcoy near Villena, in April. The townspeople dress up in Moorish and Christian costumes and re-enact the battles that took place in the region during the period of the Reconquest. Both of these spectacles are unique.

During the Fallas, massive firework displays and bonfires light up the night sky above the city of Valencia.

The Islands – the Balearics and Canaries

Neither the Balearics, off the Catalonian coast, nor the Canaries, near the coast of north-west Africa, produce outstanding wines today. Despite their long traditions – Canary wine is referred to by Shakespeare, for example – both industries are in a sad state of decline. The reasons are twofold: on both island groups there is enormous pressure from the tourist industry; and although the Balearics are fertile, in the Canaries the viticultural conditions are almost unbelievably harsh. Under this sort of pressure, the area devoted to vines has increasingly dwindled. In Mallorca, for example, chief of the Balearic islands, the vineyards have been reduced from over 27,000 hectares to a mere 4,000. Neither the Balearics nor the Canaries has a D.O.C. wine.

With their large influx of tourists, both island groups are net importers of wine. In fact, finding unadulterated local wine is surprisingly difficult in either area.

The Balearics

The Balearic group consists of Mallorca (Majorca), Minorca, Ibiza and Formentera, and lesser islands. Today, Mallorca is the only one that produces sizeable quantities of wine. Production is concentrated around Binisalem, in the centre, where the plantings are mainly of the red Manto Negro, and to the South in Felanitx, an area planted mostly with the Fogoneu. The resulting wines are very different: the Manto Negro produces dark wines that are big in body and can reach an alcoholic strength of 15 to 16 per cent; the Fogoneu, produces light, fresh and fruity rosés. Much of the wine is made by small grape farmers.

The larger firm of José L. Ferrer in Binisalem, however, produces some good wines, young and fruity reds, and a Gran Reserva with six-year oak ageing.

The Canaries

With hot winds blowing from the Sahara, volcanic terrain, and little to no rainfall, viticulture in the Canary Islands is very difficult indeed. The vines survive on the dew, which is absorbed by the porous volcanic stone. In Lanzarote, each vine has to be planted in a pit sometimes up to 3 metres (12 ft) deep or protected from the burning wind by stone walls. It is not surprising then that wines from the Canaries are costly.

Four of the group's seven islands are still producing wine, although not as much as they used to. In terms of volume, Tenerife is the most important. Here the vineyards are planted on the northern side of the island around the towns of Icod de los Vinos, Tacoronte and Orotava, producing reds and whites with a moderate to high level of alcohol. On La Palma, the vineyards are planted in the southern tip, near the village of Fuencaliente, and produce some reasonable dry and big-bodied *claretes*. On Gran Canaria, they are planted around Santa Brígida.

The best wines are produced on Lanzarote, where viticulture is the most difficult. Made from the Malvasía and the Listán and aged for a few months in 600-litre oak casks, they are amber coloured, big-bodied wines with a pungent, perfumed nose and a level of alcohol that puts them halfway between a table and a dessert wine. Those to look out for are produced by Bodegas Mozaga and El Grifo.

Glossary of Wine and Food Terms

Aguardiente a fiery transparent spirit distilled from vegetables.

Ajo garlic.

Albariza the white soil of Jerez, with a high limestone content.

Alcachofa artichoke.

Allioli a popular sauce in Catalonia made from garlic and olive oil.

Amontillado a type of sherry or Montilla.

Arroz rice.

Asado a roast.

Asador a restaurant that specializes in roasted meats.

Bacalao cod.

Barrica the classic 225–litre oak barrel, usually made of oak.

Bodega a winery or wine cellar.

Bodeguero the owner or manager of a bodega.

Brut or **Brut nature** a dry CAVA.

Butifarra type of sausage particularly popular in Catalonia and the Balearics.

Cachelada a stew.

Caldereta a stew, or the pot it is cooked in.

Callos tripe.

Capataz a master taster in Jerez.

CAVA a sparkling wine made by the *méthode champenoise*.

Cava a cellar.

Chilindrón a type of sauce made from peppers, tomatoes and garlic, popular in Aragon, Navarra and the Rioja.

Chorizo a spicy sausage not unlike the French *saucisson*.

Chuleta a chop. A **chuletón** is larger.

Clarete a light red wine usually made with a mixture of red and white grapes.

Cochinillo suckling pig.

Codorniz quail.

Conejo rabbit.

Consejo Regulador the Regulating Council of a Denomination of Origin, which enforces strict standards of quality and authenticity.

Copita the traditional slender sherry glass, tapered in towards the mouth.

Cordero lamb.

Cosecha vintage.

Coupage a blend of wines or grape varieties.

Cream a type of sherry or Montilla.

Criadera an oak butt used in the *solera* system.

Crianza a wine that has been aged in oak barrel.

Degüelle the disgorging process used for sparkling wines.

Dorada type of fish popular in the Levante.

Dorado a fortified golden wine made in Rueda.

Dulce sweet. Also used for a sweet type of CAVA.

Estofado a stew.

Fino type of dry sherry or Montilla.

Flor a layer of yeasts formed inside the butt of sherry or Montilla on the surface of the wine.

Fondillón a rare matured wine made in the southern Levante.

Garnatxa d'Emporda a sweet dessert wine made in the Ampurdan.

Gazpacho in Andalusia this is a cold vegetable soup; in the Levante and La Mancha it is a hearty stew.

Generoso a fortified *apéritif* or dessert wine.

Gran Reserva a wine matured for many years in barrel and bottle.

GRANVAS a sparkling wine made by the Cuve Clos method.

133

Habas broad beans.
Horno (de asar) an oven.

Jamón ham.
Judias beans: *judias blancas* are haricot beans; *judias negras* are runner beans.

Lágrima a sweet wine made from the free-run must of the grapes.
Licor de Tiraje a sweet wine added to sparkling wines in different measures to achieve different levels of sweetness.

Manzanilla a very dry sherry made in Sanlúcar de Barrameda.
Masia a country house or winery in Catalonia.
Méthode champenoise the superior method of making sparkling wines, from Champagne – the second fermentation takes place within the bottle, as opposed to tanks.
Migas breadcrumbs or flour fried in olive oil.
Morcilla a black sausage, akin to black pudding.
Moscatel a sweet dessert wine made from the Moscatel grape.
Must grape juice before fermentation.

Négociant wine broker.

Olla a stewing pot.
Oloroso a type of sherry or Montilla.

Paella the famous dish from the Levante made with meat, fish, vegetables and rice.
Pale Cream a type of sherry or Montilla.
Pálido pale. Also used for a fortified wine from Rueda.
Palo Cortado a rare type of sherry.
Parrillada a grill popular in Catalonia.

Patatas potatoes.
Pato duck.
Perdiz partridge.
Pétillant slightly sparkling or effervescent.
Phylloxera a louse that attacks and destroys the roots of the vine. The European industry has defeated it by grafting its stock on to resistant American rootstock.
Picada a sauce made with saffron, garlic, nuts, parsley and cinnamon.
Pimiento pepper.
Pinchito a small kebab usually served as a *tapa*.

Rancio an old white wine that has been matured and allowed to oxidize in barrel.
Rape hake.
Removido the turning process used for sparkling wine. The bottles are gradually turned upside down so that the sediment settles on the cork, prior to its removal by *degüelle*.
Reserva a wine that has been matured in barrel and bottle.
Revuelto de Setas a mushroom omelette.
Romesco a type of sauce made with garlic, tomatoes, peppers, bread and almonds, very popular in Catalonia.
Rosado rosé wine.
Rovellón a type of wild mushroom found in Catalonia.

Samfaina a sauce made with aubergines, tomatoes, onions, and courgettes.
Sangría a drink made with wine, brandy and fruit.
Seco dry. Also used to describe a dryish sort of CAVA.
Sofrito a sauce of sautéed onions, tomatoes, peppers and garlic in olive oil.
Solera system the system used in the

Grape Varieties

production of sherry, Montilla and Malaga. The *solera* is the butt of wine at ground level; the upper butts are known as *criaderas*.

Tannin a substance in the grape pips and stalks which gives the wine its backbone and staying power, enabling it to last longer.

Tapas small dishes or appetizers served with drinks at a bar.

Ternera veal.

Tinaja large earthenware amphora-shaped containers in which wine is stored.

Torta a hard flour biscuit served with Gazpacho Manchego.

Tortilla an omelette.

Trucha trout.

Varietal wine made from a single grape variety.

Vendimia grape harvest.

Vendimiador grape picker.

Venencia a small thin silver cup attached to a whalebone; it is used by the *venenciador* to extract samples from the sherry butts and pour them into glasses.

Vi de l'any a Catalan wine, particularly from the Ampurdán, released just a few months after fermentation.

Vino wine.

Vino de aguja 'needle' wine, a wine with a slight *pétillance*.

Vino de l'año a wine intended to be consumed within a year of the harvest.

Vino del cosechero a wine produced by a small grape farmer, usually sold by the jug or demijohn.

Zarzuela a fish stew, particularly popular in Catalonia.

Zurracapote a wine mixed with fruit and cinnamon.

The following varieties are the principal grapes used in Spanish wines:

Airén (white). The principal variety of Castilla La Mancha (and one of the most widely planted varieties in the world), the Airén can produce pleasant, light and fruity young whites which are often rather neutral.

Bobal (black). A hardy vine planted mostly in the Levante. Its wines tend to oxidize quickly, but it can produce good rosés, particularly those from Utiel-Requena.

Cabernet Sauvignon (black). One of the world's great travellers, and now one of the most popular imported 'noble' varieties in Spain, planted increasingly in Navarra and Catalonia. South of the Pyrenees it produces enormous wines that are packed with colour, fruit and tannin, and thus are often blended with softer grape varieties.

Cariñena (black). Also known as the Mazuelo, and widely planted in Aragon (with smaller pockets in the Rioja and Catalonia). It produces wines that are deep in colour, dry and with a high degree of alcohol and extract.

Chardonnay (white). Another favourite import, particularly well liked in Catalonia. In Spain it can produce some almost overpoweringly fruity and intense wines, but it is usually used in blends, to add touches of finesse and depth to both still wines and CAVAs.

Garnacha (black). An indigenous Spanish variety known in France as the Grenache, this is now the most widely planted black variety in Spain, particularly in Navarra, the Rioja and Aragon. When well vinified, it produces excellent, open and very fruity wines, so it is ideal for young reds and rosés. Its biggest weakness is its lack of tannin and staying power.

Graciano (black). Planted in small parcels in the Rioja Alta, it produces wines with good staying power, delicate aroma and flavour. Unfortunately, it is usually blended, but it can make a good blend into a really great one.

Macabeo. See Viura.

Malvasía (white). Planted in increasingly small parcels in the Rioja and Navarra and the Canaries. It produces wines of character, with good body and aroma.

Mazuelo. See Cariñena.

Merseguera (white). Planted widely in the Levante, particularly Valencia. Its pale wines can be fresh and fruity, but they tend to lack charm.

Monastrell (black). Again, a favourite variety in the Levante, particularly in the southern part of the region, where it produces wines that are big in body, dry, high in alcohol, and long lasting.

Palomino (white). The great variety of Jerez, the Palomino produces wines which lack character and are low in sugar and acidity. It is the *solera* system that transforms the unremarkable wines into excellent sherries.

Parellada (white). This is the best white variety in Catalonia, and particularly the Penedès, where it produces wines of great freshness and crispness, with good fruit and aroma.

Pedro Ximénez (white). Widely planted in Montilla, and used in Jerez to make sweetening wines. It produces fairly neutral wines with a high level of alcohol (not surprisingly, considering the southern sun). Again, it is the *solera* system that transforms the wine.

Tempranillo (black). Also known as the Ull de Llebre in Catalonia, and as the Cencibel in New Castile. The Tinto Fino of Old Castile is a close variant. Usually considered to be the best native black variety in Spain, it is planted in increasing quantities all over the country. In the Rioja and Navarra it produces wines with good aroma, fruit and colour, and a moderate level of alcohol – qualities that are enhanced further south in New Castile, where the alcohol level can reach 14 to 15 percent. It blends well with the Garnacha, which adds extra fruit and alcohol; the Tempranillo provides the elegance and finesse.

Tinto Fino. See Tempranillo.

Ull de Llebre. See Tempranillo.

Verdejo (white). A native of Old Castile, increasingly planted in Rueda. Verdejo is capable of producing wines of elegance, crisp, well-balanced, fruity and characterful.

Viura (white). Also known as the Macabeo, and planted in the Rioja, Navarra, Catalonia and the Levante. Its wines are crisp, fruity and with good aroma, but they often lack character.

Xarel.lo (white). The third variety of the Penedès, this grape produces wines that can be coarse, but they have body, acidity and a relatively high level of alcohol.

Spanish Vintages

Spain has more hectares under vine than any other country in Europe, and the grapes are grown in climatic conditions that vary considerably: the conditions in Jerez, for example, could not be more different than those in, say, the Ribera del Duero. It is therefore always difficult to generalize about Spain's vintages.

In general, however, a distinction may be made between those regions that are influenced by the Mediterranean, and those in the southern part of the country (namely Catalonia, New Castile, the Levante and Andalusia), and those that are influenced by the Atlantic (namely Navarra, the Rioja, Old Castile and Galicia). In the former regions the climate is generally consistent, and produces crops that vary little in quality or quantity, except in very exceptional years such as 1988, when a combination of late frosts, hail storms, and mildew (caused by an unusually wet summer) reduced the yield dramatically. In the Atlantic regions, the climate is less consistent, and both the quality and the quantity of the *vendimias* vary considerably.

It must also be noted that, traditionally, Spanish red wines are only released when they are ready for drinking, in contrast to, for example, Bordeaux or Burgundy. And again in contrast to the wines of these two great French regions, Spanish wines tend to reach a plateau comparatively early, and then to stay on it for several years.

The following vintage chart for Spain's four leading quality regions has been compiled from the reports of the Consejos Reguladores, which classify their vintages from 'excellent' to 'poor' (though the latter category is rarely used). As most Spanish white wines are now made to drink early, this chart is limited to red wines only.

Note: this is a general guide; unfortunately there can always be exceptions.

	Rioja	Navarra	Penedès	Ribera del Duero
1970	VG	E	VG	G
1971	P	P	G	VG
1972	P	P	E	A
1973	G	E	VG	E
1974	G	G	G	G
1975	VG	G	VG	G
1976	G	G	E	VG
1977	A	A	G	P
1978	VG	VG	E	G
1979	A	A	A	VG
1980	G	A	VG	G
1981	VG	E	VG	VG
1982	E	E	VG	E
1983	G	VG	G	G
1984	A	VG	VG	A
1985	G	G	VG	G
1986	G	G	G	G
1987	VG	VG	E	A/G

Symbols

E excellent
VG very good
G good
A average
P poor.

Older vintages to look out for (although they are increasingly hard to find, even in Spain) include the following:
1969 (Penedès); 1968 (all regions); 1966 (Penedès); 1964 (all regions; this year amounts to a legend in the Rioja); 1963 (Penedès); and 1962 and 1961 (the Rioja).

Further Information

METRIC EQUIVALENTS		
Kilometres		**Miles**
1.61	1	0.62
3.22	2	1.24
4.83	3	1.86
6.44	4	2.49
8.05	5	3.11
9.66	6	3.73
11.27	7	4.35
12.88	8	5.59
14.48	9	5.59
64.37	10	6.21
80.47	50	31.07
96.56	60	37.28
112.65	70	43.50
128.75	80	49.71
144.84	90	55.92
160.93	100	62.14

Hectares		**Acres**
0.41	1	2.47
0.81	2	4.94
1.21	3	7.41
1.62	4	9.88
2.02	5	12.36
2.43	6	14.83
2.83	7	17.30
3.24	8	19.77
3.64	9	22.24
4.05	10	24.71
8.09	20	49.42
12.14	30	74.13
16.19	40	98.84
20.23	50	123.56
24.28	60	148.26
28.33	70	172.97
32.37	80	197.68
36.42	90	222.40
40.47	100	247.11

Information on wine

If you are British-based, Wines from Spain, a wine information and promotion bureau in London, can be very helpful for advice, addresses and general information:
Wines from Spain 22 Manchester Square, London W1M 5AP. Tel: (01) 935 6140. The bureau also publishes useful leaflets.

Consejos Reguladores

Alternatively, when you are in Spain, the Consejos Reguladores for each Denomination of Origin can prove helpful, and they also provide information leaflets. It must be stressed, however, that these organizations are generally very busy, and they do not often have English speakers on their staff.
Alella Calle Rector 22, Alella (Barcelona). Tel: (93) 330 6451.
Alicante Pintor Aparico 17, Alicante. Tel: (965) 22 78 42.
Almansa Mandez Nuñez 5, Almansa (Albacete). Tel: (967) 34 02 58.
Ampurdán-Costa Brava Plaza Cataluña 5, Figueras (Gerona). Tel: (972) 50 41 92.
Campo de Borja Barrio Curto 2, Ainzón (Zaragoza). Tel: (976) 86 88 06. Cariñena Calle Mayor 30, Cariñena (Zaragoza). Tel: (976) 62 06 94.
CAVA and other Sparkling Wines Av. de Tarragona 24, Vilafranca del Penedès (Barcelona). Tel: (93) 890 31 04.
Jumilla Calle San Roque 15, Jumilla (Murcia). Tel: (968) 78 17 61.
La Mancha Estación de Viticultura y Enologia, Cañalejas 15, Alcázar de San Juan (Ciudad Real). Tel: (926) 54 05 37.
Málaga Edificio Administrativo de Servicio Multiple, Av. de la Aurora 47, Málaga. Tel: (952) 32 95 00.
Montilla Ronda de los Tejares 24, Córdoba. Tel: (957) 22 54 84.
Navarra Conde Oliveto 2, Pamplona (Navarra). Tel: (948) 22 78 52.
Penedès Amalia Soler 27, Vilafranca del Penedès (Barcelona). Tel: (93) 890 02 11.
Priorato Pasco Sunyer s/n, Estación Enológica, Reus (Tarragona). Tel: (977) 31 20 32.
Ribeiro Calle Oliveira s/n, Rivadavia (Orense). Tel: (988) 47 10 15.
Ribera del Duero Plaza Primo de Rivera 3, Aranda de Duero (Burgos). Tel: (947) 50 56 06.
Rioja Jorge Vigán 51, Logroño. Tel: (941) 23 15 38.
Rueda Santísimo Cristo 26, Rueda (Valladolid). Tel: (983) 86 82 48.
Sherry Av. Alvaro Domecq s/n, Jerez de la Frontera (Cádiz). Tel: (956) 33 20 50.
Somontano Pasaje Las Claras 2, Barbastro (Huesca). Tel: (974) 31 30 31.
Tarragona Av. Cataluña s/n, Tarragona. Tel: (977) 21 79 31.
Terra Alta Av. de Cataluña 5, Gandesa (Tarragona). Tel: (977) 42 01 46.
Toro Plaza de España 7, Toro (Zamora). Tel: (988) 69 03 35.
Utiel-Requena Sevilla 12, Utiel (Valencia). Tel: (962) 17 10 62.
Valdeorras Calle Dr Perez Lista 12, El Barco de Valdeorras (Orense). Tel (988) 32 03 18.
Valdepeñas Buen Suceso 14, Estación de Viticultura y Enologia, Valdepeñas (Ciudad Real). Tel: (926) 32 27 88.
Valencia Micer Masco 7, Valencia. Tel: (96) 60 20 13.
Yecla Calle Corredera 14, Yecla (Murcia). Tel: (968) 79 23 52.

Tourist offices

Spain receives some 50 million foreign tourists each year (most of whom stay in the coastal resorts) and there are tourist offices in most of its major towns. These can be useful for local information, and they will usually be able to provide the traveller with a great variety of useful information such as town maps, lists of local hotels and Paradors, youth hostels, and so forth. If you are based in the U.K., the Spanish Tourist Office can provide the addresses of local tourist offices in Spain:

The Spanish National Tourist Office Metro House, 57/58 St James's St, London SW1. Tel: (01) 499 0901. Otherwise, for the same information, there is a large central office in Madrid:

Oficina Nacional de Turismo Princesa I, Torre de Madrid, Madrid. Tel: (91) 241 23 25.

British Consulates

At present, the British government has consulates in the following cities (all close to the prime tourist areas): Alicante; Barcelona; Bilbao; Ibiza; Las Palmas; Madrid; Málaga; Palma de Mallorca; Seville; Tarragona; and Santa Cruz (on Tenerife).

Their addresses can be found in the local telephone directories, listed under the heading 'Consulado de la Gran Bretaña' or 'Consulado del Reino Unido'. Otherwise, the national or local tourist offices should be able to provide them.

Travelling from the U.K., air and ferry services, car hire

Both British Airways and Iberia operate regular scheduled flights to Alicante, Barcelona, Bilbao, Madrid, Málaga, Palma (Balearics) and Seville (usually with a stop at Valencia), and Valencia itself. For details contact either:
Iberia 169 Regent St, London W1. Tel: (01) 437 562, or **British Airways**.

Most of the major airports have offices belonging to the major hire companies, such as Hertz, Avis, Europcar and the Spanish company Atesa. Car hire tends to cost about the same as in the U.K.

Alternatively, there is a car ferry service that sails from Plymouth to Santander, about twice a week on average. It takes about 24 hours port-to-port. For details contact:
Brittany Ferries Millbay Docks, Plymouth. Tel: 0752 22 13 21.

Hotels and Paradors

See page 14.

Camping and caravans

Though perfectly legal, rough camping or the parking of caravans outside recognized sites is frowned upon by the authorities, and can be dangerous. In fact, Spain has numerous camping sites (over 350) and, although the great majority are to be found along the coast, some of them are in wonderful inland locations. For a list of sites and further information or advice, either contact the local Tourist Office, or:
International Camping Federation (IZV) Edificio España, Plaza de España, Madrid. Tel: (91) 242 10 89. It is perhaps worth repeating that some of the routes described in the course of this book (particularly the tour of the Priorato and the interior of Levante) are not recommended for caravan travel.

METRIC EQUIVALENTS		
Litres		**Imperial Gallons**
4.55	1	0.22
9.09	2	0.44
13.64	3	0.66
18.18	4	0.88
22.73	5	1.10
27.28	6	1.32
31.82	7	1.54
36.37	8	1.76
40.91	9	1.98
45.46	10	2.20
90.92	20	4.40
136.38	30	6.60
181.84	40	8.80
227.30	50	11.00
272.76	60	13.20
318.22	70	15.40
363.68	80	17.60
409.14	90	19.80
454.60	100	22.00
Litres		**U.S. Gallons**
3.79	1	0.26
7.57	2	0.53
11.36	3	0.79
15.14	4	1.06
18.93	5	1.32
22.71	6	1.59
26.50	7	1.85
30.28	8	2.11
34.07	9	2.38
37.85	10	2.64
75.71	20	5.28
113.56	30	7.92
151.41	40	10.56
189.27	50	13.21
227.12	60	15.85
264.97	70	18.49
302.82	80	21.13
340.68	90	23.78
378.53	100	26.42

Province codes

Alava	45
Albacete	67
Alicante	65
Almeria	51
Andorra	738
Asturias	85
Avila	18
Badajoz	24
Balearics	71
Barcelona	3
Burgos	47
Cáceres	27
Cádiz	56
Cantabria	42
Castellón	64
Ceuta	56
Ciudad Real	26
Córdoba	57
La Coruña	81
Cuenca	66
Gerona	72
Granada	58
Guadalajara	11
Guipuzcoa	43
Huelva	55
Huesca	74
Jaen	53
León	87
Lérida	73
Lugo	82
Madrid	1
Málaga	52
Melilla	52
Murcia	68
Navarra	48
Orense	88
Palencia	88
Las Palmas	28
Pontevedra	86
La Rioja	41
Salamanca	23
Santa Cruz (Tenerife)	22
Segovia	11
Sevilla	54
Soria	75
Tarragona	77
Teruel	74
Toledo	25
Valencia	6
Valladolid	83
Vizcaya	94
Zamora	88
Zaragoza	76

Public holidays

Virtually every town and city in Spain celebrates the feast day of its patron saint and, if this day happens to be one day away from the weekend, the day in between also becomes a holiday (known as a *puente* or bridge). Most of the bodegas will close, so it is very important to get information on local holidays from the local Tourist Office as soon as you can. In addition, there are the following national holidays:

January 1 (New Year)
January 6 (Epiphany)
March 19 (St Joseph)
End March/early April Maundy Thursday, Good Friday, Easter Monday (Easter usually amounts to an extended holiday)
May 1 (Labour Day)
Corpus Christi (the second Thursday after Whitsun)
July 25 (St James the Apostle)
August 15 (Assumption)
October 12 (Our Lady of El Pilar)
November 1 (All Saints' Day)
December 8 (Immaculate Conception)
December 25 (Christmas and New Year tend to become an extended holiday)

Using the telephone in Spain

Public telephones are preferable to those in hotel rooms, which are very expensive to use. The public telephones also give clear pictorial instructions for their use.

Each Spanish province has its code number (as listed). To phone a number in another province you must dial 9 and then the appropriate provincial code. (For example, to phone a number in the province of Barcelona when you are outside the province, dial 93 [prefix and code], followed by the number.) You don't need the code if you are phoning a number within the same province.

Sample letter to a bodega owner

[Sender's name, address and telephone number, and date]

Muy Señores Nuestros: Hemos leido en la *Travellers Wine Guide – Spain* publicada por Waymark. aqui en el Reino Unido que acceptan visitas del público. Estaremos en su región el día [day] de [month] de este año y nos gustaría, si es conveniente, visitar su bodega a las [time]. Esperamos que estarán dispuestos a recibirnos en esta fecha pero nos pondremos en contacto con ustedes por teléfono cuando llegemos a su región para confirmar nuestra visita.

Agradeciéndoles de antemano su muy amable atención les saluda muy atentamente,

[signature]

(*Translation*)

Dear Sirs,

We have read in *The Travellers Wine Guide – Spain* published by Waymark here in the U.K. that you accept visits from the public. We will be in your area on the [day] of [month] this year and would like to visit your winery at [time]. We hope that you will be able to receive us at this time and date, but will be in contact with you by telephone to confirm our visit once we have arrived in your area.

Thanking you in advance for your kind attention, yours faithfully,

Further Reading

Travel and hotel guides
Guia Campsa (revised frequently). A guide to the country's best hotels and restaurants, published by Spain's national petrol company, available in airports and bookshops in Spain. In Spanish.

Guia Oficial de Hoteles (revised frequently). A guide to Spain's hotels, Paradors and restaurants, published by the Spanish Tourist Office, available from Tourist Offices. In Spanish.

The Michelin Tourist Guide to Spain (revised frequently). Excellent for up-to-date information.

The Rough Guide to Spain (Routledge & Kegan Paul, revised frequently). An excellent guide to off-beat travel in Spain, well-researched.

Spanish cuisine
Casas, Penelope *Food and Wine in Spain* (Penguin Books).

Torres, Marimar *The Spanish Table* (Ebury Press, UK/Doubleday USA).

More difficult to find but well worth the search is D. E. Pohren's *The Wines and Folk Food of Spain*, published by the Society of Spanish Studies (Finca Espartero, Morón de la Frontera, Sevilla, Spain) in 1972. This gives a wonderful taste of a Spain that is fast disappearing, but the book is now sadly out of date.

Spanish wines
Read, Jan *The Century Companion to the Wines of Spain and Portugal* (Century Hutchinson).

Read, Jan *Pocket Guide to the Wines of Spain and Portugal* (Mitchell Beazley).

Read, Jan *Wines of the Rioja* (Sotheby's Publications).

These are the three best volumes written by the U.K.'s leading writer on Spanish wines.

Also recommended:

Duijker, Hubrecht *Wines of Rioja* (Mitchell Beazley). Readable, detailed, well-researched.

Jeffs, Julian *Sherry* (Faber & Faber). The classic work on sherry.

Lord, Tony *The New Wines of Spain* (Christopher Helm). Highly readable.

For a more technical and trade-oriented introduction to the Spanish wine industry:

Begg, Desmond *Wine Buyers Guides – SPAIN 1988* (Wine Buyers Guides).

Otherwise, for up-to-date developments in the Spanish wine industry, consult the Spanish Wines Supplement published annually by the consumer magazine *Decanter* at Priory House, 8 Battersea Park Rd, London SW8.

Writers' travel books
The following more personal and general accounts of Spain make excellent travelling companions:

Brenan, Gerald *South from Granada*, and *The Spanish Labyrinth* (Cambridge University Press). Both books are well worth reading – the first in particular is a marvellous description of village life near Granada in the 1920s and 1930s.

Hemingway, Ernest *Death in the Afternoon* (Penguin Books). One of the most fascinating books to have been written about Spain by an outsider.

Lee, Laurie *As I Walked Out One Midsummer's Morning*, and *A Rose for Winter* (Penguin Books). Beautifully written books relating the writer's travels in Spain in the 1930s and 1950s, giving a lovely glimpse of the country in those two decades.

Morris, Jan *Spain* (Penguin Books). A favourite book, beautifully written and very readable.

Index

Page references in *italic type*
indicate illustrations.

AGE Bodegas Unidas, 34
aguardiente, 64
Aguilar de la Frontera, 78, 81, *81*
Ainzón, 44
Airén grape, 64, 65, 72, 78, 135
Alavesas, Bodegas, 35
Albariño, 61
albariza, 80, 87
Albillo grape, 48, 49, 50
Alcázar de San Juan, 62, 69, *74-5*
Alcoy, 131
Alejandro Fernández, Bodegas, 50, 51
Alella, 102, 104, 117
Alella Vinícola Soc. Co-op., 104
Alfaro, 23, 30
Alfonso Abellán, 126
Alicante, 121, *126*, 127, 129
Almagro, 70, *71*
Almansa, 118, 121, *125*, 125-6
Almonacid de la Sierra, 44, *44-5*
Alvear S.A., 78, *80*, 81
Amontillado, 80, 86, 87
Ampurdán-Costa Brava, 98, 102-3
Andalusia, 76-97
Antequera, 82, *82*
Antonio Barbadillo, 94, *95*
Antonio Mestres Sagües, 110
Aragon, 42-5
Aranda de Duero, 50
Aranjuez, 62, 67, *68*
Arcos de la Frontera, 85
Arnedo, 31
asadores, 20
Asencio Cardelén, Bodegas, 128, *128*
Augusto Egli, 124
autopista, 13
Ayegui, 22
Ayuso, Bodegas, 70

Baja Montaña, 18
Baladí grape, 78
Balbino Lacosta, Heredad, 44
Balearics, 132
Barbastro, 44, 45
Barcelona, 105, *105*
Barco, 61
Bardón, Bodegas, 23
Barril, Masía, 114
Batalla del Vino, 41, *41*
Bellmunt del Priorato, 114
Berberana, Bodegas, 36-7
Bilbainas, Bodegas, 39
Binisalem, 132
Bobal grape, 120, 124, 135
bodegas, 14-15

Bordejé, Bodegas, 44
Borja, 44
brandy, 88, 89, 93
bullfighting, 59, *74-5*
Buñol, 124

C.V.C., 11
C.V.N.E. (Compañía Vinícola del Norte de España), 38, 39
Cabernet Sauvignon grape, 18, 45, 49, 50, 65, 135
Cadaqués, 102, 116
Cádiz, 90
Caino grape, 61
Calahorra, *30*, 31
Cambados, 61
Camilo Castilla, Hermanos, 23
camping, 139
Campo de Borja, 44
Campo de Criptana, *70*
Campo Viejo, Bodegas, 32, 33
Canaries, 132
Capmany, 103
caravans, 139
Carbonell, 81, *81*
Cariñena, 44-5
Cariñena grape (Mazuelo), 29, 44, 102, 135
Carricas, Bodegas, 23
Casaseca de las Chanas, 52
Castaño, Bodegas, 127
Castellers, 117, *117*
Castile, *see* New Castile; Old Castile
Catalonia, *15*, 98-117
CAVA, 100, 101, *101*, 102, 106-7, 108-9, 111
Cavas del Ampurdán, 103
Cecilio, Celler, 114
Cencibel grape, 64, 65, 72, 73, 120, 124, 136
Cenicero, 36-7
Chardonnay grape, 19, 45, 102, 107, 135
Chaves, Bodegas, 61
cheese, Manchego, 73
Chenin Blanc grape, 102
Cherubino Valsangiacomo, 123
Chiva, 124
Cigales, 48
Cintruénigo, 23
claretes, 73
Codorníu, *15*, 101, 109, *109*, 110
Conca de Barbera, 101
Consejos Reguladores, 10, 11, 133, 138
Consuegra, 68
consulates, 139
co-operatives, 14, 19
copita, 87
Córdoba, 78-9, *78-9*
Corella, 22, 23
Corral, Bodegas, 35
Costa Brava, *see* Ampurdán-Costa Brava
Costa de la Luz, 85
Costa del Sol, 85
Costers del Segre, 101
cream sherry, 80, 87

criadera, 88
Crianza Castilla la Vieja, Bodegas de, 54, 55
crocus sativus, 68
Croft, *see* Rancho Croft

De Muller, 112
degüelle, 109
Delgado Zuleta, 95
Denominaciónes de Origen, 11
Día de la Rosa del Azafrán, 68
Domecq, *see* Pedro Domecq
Duff Gordon, 93, *93*

El Bierzo, 48
El Bosque (National Park), 85
Elciego, 35-6
El Grao, *120*, 122, 123
El Grifo, Bodegas, 132
El Masnou, 98
El Toboso, 69
Embalse de Embarcaderos, 125
Enrique Ochoa Palao, 127, *127*
Escorial, 57
Espolla, 103
Estella, 22

Fábregas, Bodegas, 44, 45
Fallas, 122, *122*, 131, *131*
Falset, 113
Fariña, Bodegas, 52-3
Faustino Rivera Ulecia, Bodegas, 31
Federico Paternina, Bodegas, 38, *38*
Felanitx, 132
Félix Solís, Bodegas, 71, 73, *73*
Fernando A. de Terry, 93
Ferret i Mateu, *see* Josep Ferret
festivals: Andalusia, 78, 97; Catalonia, 117; Levante, 131; Navarra, 24; New Castile, 68; Old Castile, 59; Rioja, 41
Figueras, 103, 116, 117
Fino, 78, 80, 86, 87
flor, 80, 88, *92*
Fogoneu grape, 132
Fondillón, 129
food: Andalusia, 96; Catalonia, 116-17; Levante, 130; Navarra, 24-5; New Castile, 74-5; Old Castile, 58-9; Rioja, 40-1
Franco-Españolas, Bodegas, 33, *33*
Freixenet, 110
Fuencaliente, 132
Fuendejalón, 44
Fuenmayor, 34

Galicia, 60-1
Gandesa, 114
García Carrión, 128
García Póveda, 127
Garnacha grape, 135-6; Aragon, 44-5; Catalonia, 102; Galicia, 61; Levante, 120; Navarra, 18, 19; New Castile, 64; Old Castile, 48, 49; Rioja, 26, 29, 30

Garnatxa d'Emporda, 102
Garvey, 92, 93
generosos, 49, 54, 54-5
girasoles, 109
Godello grape, 61
Gonzalez Byass, *89*, 90, 92-3
Graciano grape, 29, 136
Gran Canaria, 132
Granada, 97
GRANVAS, 109
Gratallops, 114
Grazalema, 85
Gurpegui, Bodegas, 31

Haro, 38-9, 41
Harvey, *see* John Harvey
Hemingway, Ernest, *20*, 85
Herencia, *69*
Hisenda Miret, Celler, 108
holidays, public, 141
hornos de asar, 56
hotels, 14
Huesca, 45

Icod de los Vinos, 132
insurance, 13
Irache, 22
Iregua river valley, *27*

Jardín del Principe, *68*
Jean León, 108
Jerez, 87
Jerez de la Frontera, 14, 88, *89*, 90-3, 97
Jesús Nazareno (co-operative), 61
John Harvey & Sons (España), 92, 93
José L. Ferrer, 132
Josep Ferret i Mateu, 108
Josep Masachs, 108, 110
Julián Chivite, Bodegas, 23
Jumilla, 120, 121, 128, 131
Juve y Camps, 110

La Aguzadera, 71
La Bleda, 110
La Invencible (co-operative), 71, 73
La Mancha, 64-5, 68-70
La Mota, *55*, 56
La Palma, 132
La Purísima (co-operative), 127
La Rioja Alta, Bodegas, 38, 39
La Seca (co-operative), 55
La Vilella Baixa, 114, 115
Laguardia, 35
Lalanne, Bodegas, 45
Lanzarote, 132
Las Campanas, *19*, 21
León, 48
Levante, 118-31
Listán grape, 132
Logroño, *32*, 32-3, 41
López Bertran, 112
López de Heredia, *35*, 39, *39*,

López Hermanos, 83, 84
López Pelayo, Bodegas, 44
Los Llanos, Bodegas, 73
Luis Caballero, 93
Luis Megía, Bodegas, 73

Macabeo grape, *see* Viura
Madrid, 66-7, *66-7*
Magallón, 44
Málaga, 82-4
Malbec grape, 49, 50
Malvasía grape, 29, 48, 132, 136
Mallorca, 132
Manto Negro grape, 132
Manzanares, 70
Manzanilla, 86, 87, 94
Manzanilla Pasada, 94
Marqués de Cáceres, Bodegas, 36, 37
Marqués de Griñon, 55
Marqués de Monistrol, 110, *110*
Marqués de Murrietta, Bodegas, 32-3
Marqués de Riscal, *29*, 35-6, *36*, 49, 54-5
Mazuelo grape, *see* Cariñena
Medina del Campo, *55*, 56
Mencia grape, 61
Méntrida, 64
Merlot grape, 45, 49, 50
Merseguera grape, 120, 124, 126, 136
meseta, 46, *62*
Mesón Terete, 38, 39, *40*
Mestres, *see* Antonio Mestres Sagües
méthode champenoise, 109
metric equivalents, 138, 139
Miguel Torres, Bodegas, 106, *106*, 108
Mollet, 103
Monastrell grape, 120, 126, 127, 136
Monclus, Bodegas, 44, 45
Monistrol de Noya, 110, 111
Monóvar, 128-9
Montecillo, Bodegas, 35
Montilla, 78-81
Montulia, Bodegas, 81
'Moors and Christians' festivals, 131
Moravia grape, 64
Moriles, 78
Moristrel grape, 45
Moscatel grape, 83, 87
Mota del Cuervo, 69
Mozaga, Bodegas, 132
Muerza, Bodegas, 31
Muga, Bodegas, 38, 39
Murchante, 23
Murcia, 95
Murua Entrena, Bodegas, 36
museums, wine: Catalonia, 103, 106, *107*, 109, 110; Jerez, 92, 93; Levante, 128; Navarra, 22; Rioja, 30, 32

Navarra, 16-25
Navarrete, 35
Negral grape (Tinto Madrid), 48
New Castile, 62-75

Nuestra Señora de Manjavacas (co-operative), 69
Nuestro Padre Jesús del Perdón (co-operative), 70

Ochoa, Bodegas, 21, 23
Olarra, Bodegas, 33
Old Castile, 46-59
Olite, *21*, 22-3
Oliveda, Bodegas, 103
Ollauri, 38
Oloroso, 78, 80, 87
Orense, 60
Orotava, 132
Osborne, *92*, 93

paella, 130
Palacio, Bodegas, 35
Palacio Remondo, Bodegas, 30
Palo Cortado, 80, 87
Palomino grape, 49, 54, 87, 88, 136
Pamplona, 20, 24, *25*
Pansa Blanca grape, 102
Paradores Nacionales, 14
Pardillo grape, 64
Parellada grape, 107, 136
Parxet, 102, 104
passports, 13
Pedraza de la Sierra, 57
Pedro Domecq, *14*, 90, *91*, 92-3
Pedro Rovira, Bodegas, 114
Pedro Ximénez grape, 78, 80, 82, 83, 87, 136
Pedrosa (J.), Bodegas, 114
Pedrosa de Duero, 50
Peñafiel, *49*, 50-1, *50-1*
Penedès, 92, *100*, 101, 106-10
Perelada, 103, *104*
Pérez Barquero, Bodegas, 81
Pesquera de Duero, 50, 51
petrol, 13
phylloxera, 28, 54, 101, 120
Pineau, Jean, 35-6
Piqueras, Bodegas, 125, 126
Planta Nova grape, 120
Pont de Molins, 103
Pontevedra, 60
Primitivo Quiles, 129
Priorato, 113-14
pueblos blancos, 85
Puente del Diablo, *112*
Puente la Reina, 21, *22*
Puerto de Santa Maria, 88, 93
Puerto Lápice, 68-9, *74*

Radiquero, 44, 45
Raimat, 111
Rancho Croft, 92
removido, 109, *110*
Requena, 124, 131; *see also* Utiel-Requena
Reus, 113
Riaza, 56, *57*

Index

Ribadavia, 60, 61
Ribeiro, 60, 61
Ribera Alta, 18
Ribera Baja, 18
Ribera del Duero, 48-9, 50-1
Ricardell, 103
Rioja, 26-41
Riojanas, Bodegas, 36, 37
Ronda, *84*, 85
rosados, 18
Rosas, 102
Rovellats, 108, 110
Rueda, 49, 53, 54-5

saffron, 68
Salvador Póveda, 129
San Adrián, 23, 31
San Fermín, 20, 24
San Isidro (co-operative), 128
San Majín, 117
San Mateo, 41
San Sadurní de Noya, 108, 109, *109*, 110
San Valero (co-operative), 44
Sandeman, 92, 93
Sanlúcar de Barrameda, 88, 94-5, *95*
Sant Martí Sarroca, 108
Santa Brígida, 132
Santa Margarita i Els Monjos, 108
Santa María de Martorelles, 104
Santiago de Compostela, 60, *61*
Santo Domingo de la Calzada, 39
Scala Dei, 114, *115*
Schenk, Bodegas, 123
Scholtz Hermanos, 83, 84
Segovia, 47, 56-7
Segura Viudas, 110
Señorio de Sarría, 21
Señorio del Contestable, Bodegas, 128
Sepúlveda, 56
Seville, 97
sherry, 78-9, 80, 86-95
'Sherry Triangle', 88, 90-5
Sitges, 107
solera system, *80*, 88, 89
Somontano, 45
Sumbilla, *16*

Tabuenca, 44
Tacoronte, 132
Tafalla, 22
tapas, 96
Tarragona, 92, 112-13, 117
telephoning in Spain, 141
Tempranillo grape, 19, 26, 29, 35, 61, 136;
    see also Cencibel; Ull de Llebre
Tenerife, 132
Terra Alta, 114
Tierra Estella, 18
Tinta de Toro grape, 48

Tinto Fino grape (Tinto del País), 48-9, 50,
    136
Tinto Madrid grape (Negral), 48
Toledo, 67
Tomás García, 78
Tomelloso, 64
Tordesillas, 52, 59
Toro, 48, 52-3
Toro de la Vega, 59
Torremilanos, Finca, 50
Torres, *see* Miguel Torres
Torrontes grape, 61, 78
tourist offices, 139
travel: in Spain, 12-13; to Spain, 139
Treixadura grape, 61

Ull de Llebre grape, 102, 136
Unión Viti-Vinícola, *see* Marqués de
    Cáceres
Utiel-Requena, 120, 121, 124-5

Valdelagrana, 93
Valdeorras, 61
Valdepeñas, 62, 64, 65, 71-3
Valdizarbe, 18
Valencia, *121*, 122-3, 131
Valladolid, 52, *53*
Valle de los Caídos, 57
Vega-Sicilia, 48, 49, 50
Vélazquez, Bodegas, 37
Verdejo grape, 49, 54-5, 136
Verdoncho grape, 64
vi de l'any, 102
Viana, 104
Vicente Gandia Pla, *123*, 124
Vilafranca del Penedès, 106, 107, 117
Vilariño-Cambados, Bodegas, 61
Villarrobledo, 70
Villena, 127
Vinícola de Castilla, 70, *72*
Vinícola Hidalgo, 94-5
Vinícola Navarra, *19*, 21
VINIVAL, Bodegas, *120*, 121, 123
vino de aguja, 48
vino del cosechero, 60
Viura grape (Macabeo), 21, 29, 64, 102,
    107, 120, 136

Williams & Humbert, 92, 93
wine: ageing, 11; classification, 10-11; labels,
    10, 11, *11*; vintages, 137

Xarel.lo grape, 102, 107, 136
Xiquets de Valls, 117

Yecla, 121, 127, 128

zurracapote, 41

ACKNOWLEDGEMENTS

Philip Clark Limited would like to thank
the following for their help in the
preparation of this book:
Tom Byers and Wine Buyers Guides
Limited for their unfailing help and advice;
J. Gillespie of Bodegas Fariña S.L.;
Laymont & Shaw Ltd for providing the
Vega-Sicilia label on page 46; Bodegas
Olarra S.A. for their help with the
illustrations for the Rioja section; the Sherry
Institute of Spain; Wines from Spain; and
Katia Cruft and Helen White for typing the
text.